A FRIENDLY GUIDE TO WOMEN IN THE NEW TESTAMENT

ROSEMARY CANAVAN

Published in Australia by
Garratt Publishing
32 Glenvale Crescent
Mulgrave, Vic. 3170

www.garrattpublishing.com.au

Copyright © Rosemary Canavan 2017
All rights reserved. Except as provided by
the Australian copyright law, no part of this
book may be reproduced in any way without
permission in writing from the publisher.

Design and typesetting by Lynne Muir

Attributions List from Creative Commons:
Page 13
© 2011 Ted, Flickr, CC BY-SA 2
St Mary Magdalene & the Risen Christ, Shkolnik
icon in St Paul Church. Dayton, OH.
Page 24-25
Creative Commons
Pic of woman anointing Jesus' feet, CC BY SA 4
Page 33
The dream of Pilates' wife by Alphonse Francois
Permission, PD-US
Images from iStockphoto on pages 5, 6, 10, 17,
20, 23, 30, 34, 37, 48.
Other photos by Rosemary Canavan.

Scripture quotations are drawn from the *New
Revised Standard Version of the Bible*, copyright
© 1989 by the Division of Christian Education of
the National Council of the Churches of Christ in
the USA.

Used by permission.
All rights reserved.

Nihil Obstat: Reverend Monsignor Peter J Kenny STD
Imprimatur: Monsignor Greg Bennet MS STL VG EV Vicar General
Date: 9 February 2017

The Nihil Obstat and Imprimatur are official
declarations that a book or pamphlet is free
of doctrinal or moral error. No implication is
contained therein that those who have granted
the Nihil Obstat and Imprimatur agree with the
contents, opinions or statements expressed.
They do not necessarily signify that the work
is approved as a basic text for catechetical
instruction.

ISBN 9781925073355

Cataloguing in Publication information for this
title is available from the National Library of
Australia. www.nla.gov.au

The author and publisher gratefully acknowledge
the permission granted to reproduce the
copyright material in this book. Every effort has
been made to trace copyright holders and to
obtain their permission for the use of copyright
material.

The publisher apologises for any errors or
omissions in the above list and would be grateful
if notified of any corrections that should be
incorporated in future reprints or editions of this
book.

CONTENTS

INTRODUCTION 3

DEDICATION 4

WOMEN IN THE GOSPELS 5
 Mary 6
 Mary Magdalene (Mary a woman of Magdala) 12
 Elizabeth 15
 Anna (Hannah in Hebrew, Hanna in Greek) 18
 Joanna 19
 Susanna 20
 Mary the mother of James (and Joses/Joseph) 21
 Mary of Clopas 21
 Martha and Mary 22
 Woman who anointed Jesus 24
 A woman healed and a daughter restored to life 26
 Samaritan woman at the well 29
 The Syrophoenician woman and the Caananite woman 31
 Peter's mother-in-law 32
 Pilate's wife 33
 Herodias and her daughter 34
 Widows 36
  Widow of Nain 36

WOMEN IN THE PAULINE LETTERS 37
 Junia 38
 Prisca (Priscilla) 39
 Phoebe 41
 Women in Rome 42
 Other Women of the Pauline Household Communities 43
  Apphia, Chloe, Euodia and Syntyche, Nympha 43

WOMEN IN ACTS 44
 Lydia 45
 Tabitha (Dorcas) 47
 Sapphira 47
 Other women in Acts 48
  Damaris, Drusilla, Bernice 48
 More women 49
  Lois and Eunice 47
  Claudia 47

CONCLUSION 50

BIBLIOGRAPHY 51

ENDNOTES 52

INTRODUCTION

A *Friendly Guide to Women in the New Testament* illuminates the women who accompanied Jesus on his mission, those he met on the way, those who appear in the letters of Paul as co-workers and members of the early communities of Christ followers and those who are encountered in the growth of the Church in Acts. These women were disciples and apostles, mothers, wives, daughters and sisters, witnesses to the resurrection, and co-workers and followers of Paul in proclaiming Christ to the Gentiles. Naturally, Mary has pride of place as the mother and first disciple of Jesus. Among these women there are some who are unnamed yet take their place as significant women of faith and witness to Jesus, such as the woman who anointed Jesus: "wherever the good news is proclaimed, what she has done will be told in remembrance of her" (Mark 15:9; Matt 26:13). To keep this true to the fullness of the New Testament, some more unlikely characters are included: Herodias and her daughter, and Sapphira.

These are all women of the first century CE living in places across the Greco-Roman world under the regime of the Roman Empire in Palestine, Asia Minor, Greece, and Rome. This is a world and time very distant from our own. To understand these women and their roles, we need to take off our shoes and walk in theirs. We need to enter their world and see with their eyes and

Byzantine icon, copy

their faith. Many are inspirational women, and yet they are also like the women of today, acting authentically to answer their call in their own world.

What we know of the women of the New Testament comes to us from the writings of men, mainly the evangelists and Paul, as well as the writers of the letters outside the Pauline corpus. The portrayals of women are not always consistent across the writings, giving different perspectives and glimpses of these women in narratives written for specific communities and purposes. Always we remember that the focus of the New Testament is Jesus. Mark's Gospel begins: "The beginning of the good news of Jesus Christ Son of God". It is the ongoing good news of the initiative of God, who gifts the world with Jesus, God's son, and the outpouring of the Holy Spirit. As we come to know the women we do so in relation to this meta-narrative. If we are disappointed that there is not more about the women, we also rejoice that they are inextricably woven into the fabric of the life and mission of Jesus from his birth to his death, as first witnesses of the resurrection and in the spread of the good news to the ends of the earth.

These are women of a particular time, whom we glimpse through cultural, political and social lenses that do not always give them voice or precedence. Sometimes there is need to imagine and read between the lines. These women continue to inspire women and men today, and they offer their legacy of faith and service to the story of the Church.

Dr Rosemary Canavan
Catholic Theological College
University of Divinity

THIS BOOK IS DEDICATED TO
ALL THE WOMEN
WHO HAVE INSPIRED,
ENCOURAGED AND JOURNEYED
WITH ME.

Cover image and right: Virgin Mary mosaic
Title page: The Mona Lisa of the Galilee from a mosaic in Sepphoris

WOMEN IN THE GOSPELS

MARY

Mary holds the hearts of believers throughout the centuries as mother and first disciple of Jesus. Muslims also hold her dear. Throughout Turkey she is held in great reverence, as is shown by the enormous statue near Mary's House in Ephesus. The tradition that surrounds Mary is very much larger than the person we discover in the New Testament. The Protoevangelium (Infancy Gospel) of James, written no earlier than the second century CE, is subtitled "The Birth of Mary the Holy Mother of God and Very Glorious Mother of Jesus Christ". It is the best known of the later texts containing legends about Mary and her birth, life, death and bodily ascension into heaven. It is this apocryphal text that recounts Joachim as Mary's father and Anna as her mother. Much of this text echoes Luke's narrative and attributes similar sayings to Mary as are noted of Jesus in the Gospel of Luke.

MEETING MARY IN THE BIRTH NARRATIVES

The Gospels of Luke and Matthew add accounts of the birth and infancy of Jesus primarily to establish who Jesus is from the beginning. These are not historical accounts. Rather, they draw on the Old Testament scriptures artfully and theologically to weave the backdrop for the arrival of the Messiah and the fulfilment of God's promise. We need to remember as we focus on Mary that she too is threaded into this backdrop. Our attention to the symbols and scriptural references will help us hear and understand these accounts in all the richness that the first audiences enjoyed.

MARY AND THE ANNUNCIATION AND BIRTH OF JESUS ACCORDING TO LUKE

Luke's Gospel, written around 85 CE, relates a divine annunciation to Mary and the birth of Jesus. Mary receives the word of God via the angel Gabriel:

> And behold, you will conceive in your womb and bear a son, and you will name him Jesus. He will be great, and will be called the Son of the Most High, and the Lord God will give to him the throne of his ancestor David. (Luke 1:31–32*)

Below: Mary's House, Ephesus, Turkey   *Right: Statue of Mary, Ephesus, Turkey*

* an asterisk denotes the author's translation

The entrance of Gabriel signifies a message from God, a divine intervention. His appearance to announce both the birth of John the Baptist to Zechariah and the birth of Jesus to Mary is met with great fear, which is the usual response before an epiphany. What we observe of Mary is her openness to the word and her willing and faithful trust to what we would imagine as an incomprehensible request. Her faithfulness to God is paramount as she humbly says yes to becoming the mother of Jesus.

Mary's pregnancy and the birth of Jesus are paralleled with Elizabeth and the birth of John the Baptist. In a beautiful centrepiece to this section of the narrative we see Elizabeth and Mary embrace as kinswomen, old and young, both with the promise of God, bearing the herald of the good news and Jesus the Messiah.

Elizabeth greets Mary with the words that have become the prayer of the faithful through the ages: "Blessed are you among women, and blessed is the fruit of your womb" (Luke 1:42). Mary responds with a canticle of praise, echoed daily in the Prayer of the Church. Luke weaves this and a number of other great songs or canticles of Israel into his narrative. This song that Mary sings as she meets Elizabeth is very similar to that sung by Hannah (1 Sam 2:1-10) when she discovers that she is pregnant. Hanna's song is in praise and thanks to God for looking after the "little people", those who are hungry or weak. Mary's song, which we know as the Magnificat, echoes these values which are the thrust of the mission of Jesus in Luke's Gospel.

> **DID YOU KNOW?**
>
> ✠ The Angel Gabriel, named only in Luke's Gospel (Luke 1:19, 26), is also mentioned in the Book of Daniel (9:20). Gabri-el in Hebrew means "the mighty one of God". (El means God.)

7

DID YOU KNOW?

✢ Today there are two traditional sites for the Shepherd's Field, not far out of Bethlehem. The Catholic site maintained by the Franciscans is remembered with a beautiful chapel designed by Antonio Barluzzi in 1954, which adjoins the ruins of a fourth century church. Not far from these are some shepherd cave chapels. The Greek Orthodox site has excavated a subterranean fourth century church with mosaic floors.

✢ In the first century, Nazareth was a village of about 500 inhabitants unlike the city of around 70,000 that it is today. Excavations next to the Basilica of the Annunciation show remains of the houses of Nazareth. Nearby in the International Centre of Mary there are remains of what is believed to be a first century house, something like the one in which Mary grew up.

Above: Nativity image from Shepherd's Field Chapel, designed by Antonio Barluzzi on the outskirts of Jerusalem

The mention of Jesus in a manger recalls a passage from Isa 1:3: "The ox knows its owner, and the donkey the manger of its master; but Israel has not known me, and my people have not understood me." (Isaiah 1:3*). In the birth narrative, faithful Israel does recognise Jesus through Elizabeth, Simeon and the shepherds. These poor, lowly and barren will also be the focus of the mission of Jesus in Luke.
Sadly, the rulers will later fulfil Isaiah's words.

Below: Mary with Anne and Joachim, Chora Church Museum, Istanbul, Turkey

It is through Luke's telling that we come close to Mary and the way that she walks as mother and disciple. We imagine her as a young Palestinian woman betrothed to be married. The annunciation is depicted in classic art works and icons that lift the story from the text and into our vision and memory. Her response to God, "Behold the servant of the Lord; let it be with me according to your word." (Luke 1:38*), abides as the faithful response to the call of God.

Having stayed with Elizabeth in her confinement, Mary returns to Nazareth, and the time for John to be born arrives with little occasion. As the time for Jesus' birth arrives, the narrative draws us away from the rural environment and sets the scene in the Roman Empire with a decree from the Emperor Augustus. Mary needs to travel with Joseph to Bethlehem, to the city of David, as Joseph is from the "house and family of David" (Luke 2:4). She will bear her child away from home and away from her kinswomen.

> And she gave birth to her firstborn son and wrapped him in bands of cloth, and laid him in a manger, because there was no place for them in the inn.
> (Luke 2:7)

These few lines do not reveal anything of the experience of the birth for Mary. This miraculous, wonderful moment is recorded without fanfare or emotion. The heavenly choir of angels will appear to the shepherds announcing the good news:

> "Do not be afraid; for see—I am bringing you good news of great joy for all the people: to you is born this day in the city of David a Saviour, who is the Messiah, the Lord." (Luke 2:10–11).

The shepherds set off and find Mary and Joseph, with Jesus lying in the manger. Whatever the conversation between shepherds and Joseph and Mary, we only have the narrator's comment: "But Mary treasured all these words and pondered them in her heart" (Luke 2:19).

When the time comes for their purification, Mary travels again with Joseph and Jesus to Jerusalem to present him to the Lord. Mary is faced with great challenges as she is told by Simeon in the Temple that her soul will be pierced with a sword. She hears this along with the acclamation of who Jesus is, and yet we have no word from her. Later, when Jesus stays behind in the Temple and his parents search desperately for him, Mary again is observed to have "treasured all these things in her heart" (Luke 2:51).

Mary's wisdom in treasuring these things also shows her trust in God. She will walk the path of the joy and heartbreak of her son in faithfulness and hope, not always understanding but pondering and treasuring all that comes with the gift of her son, Jesus.

MARY AND THE BIRTH OF THE MESSIAH ACCORDING TO MATTHEW

In contrast, Matthew's account of Jesus' birth emphasises Joseph. God's word comes to Joseph in a dream. Mary has no word in this. She is the wife of Joseph and the means for the birth of the Messiah. Mary travels to Bethlehem with Joseph and bears the child. The larger narrative fills in the details of the star that guides the Magi (wise men), the Magis' encounter with King Herod and the need for Joseph, Mary and Jesus to flee to Egypt. In Matthew, the Magi enter the house, where they find "the

DID YOU KNOW?

✚ Matthew's account has deep echoes in the Old Testament. This enables Matthew to portray Jesus as a prophet like Moses and as the fulfilment of the ancient prophecies.

✚ Jesus is revealed to be like Moses through the patterning of his birth narrative on the story of Moses' birth. Jesus is saved from Herod's decree for all the boys under two to be slaughtered just as Moses is saved from the Pharaoh who orders all the baby boys be killed (Exod 1:22).

✚ The portrayal of Joseph recalls the figure of Joseph, son of Jacob, who was a man of dreams (Gen 40), who protected his family and brought them to Egypt (Gen 46).

✚ When Moses led Israel out from Egypt he met a Magus (wiseman) who spoke of a star rising from Israel, which is symbolic of a future king: "I see him, but not now; I behold him, but not near—a star shall come out of Jacob, and a sceptre shall rise out of Israel;" (Numbers 24:17a).

child with Mary his mother" (Matt 2:11). Here Mary is silent, and there is only imagination to fill in the gaps.

MARY ON THE ROAD WITH JESUS

In the Gospel of John, Mary is only identified as "Mother of Jesus".[1] She is there with Jesus at beginning and end of his ministry. At Cana she initiates the action, advising him at the wedding of the lack of wine. She encourages the servants "Do whatever he tells you" (John 2:5). Jesus protests that his "hour" has not yet come. Yet Mary believes that he will intervene, and he does. The abundance of wine is the first sign that reveals the identity of Jesus and his disciples believe (John 2:11). After this event, Jesus, his mother and the disciples go to Capernaum. We observe that a household of believers is forming around Jesus (John 2:12).

Beyond this, there is little mention of Mary on the road with Jesus. When Jesus is rejected in his hometown, we hear that the locals recognise him as the son of Mary (Matt 13:55; Mark 6:3; John 6:42). In Luke we hear, "And he was told, 'Your mother and your brothers are standing outside, wanting to see you'" (Luke 8:20). Jesus' response seems unkind as he tells those assembled, "My mother and my brothers are those who hear the word of God and do it" (Luke 8:21). On this occasion his words affirm that his mother and brothers are models. Similar accounts in Matthew and Mark are not so inclusive, recounting Jesus indicating to those in front of him that they are his mother and brothers (Matt 12:49; Mark 3:34).

The presence of Mary at Cana and Capernaum and then later outside a place where Jesus was teaching gives an indication that she was in touch with him and following

Above: Crucifixion icon with Mary and John

his mission. She enters John's narrative again at the cross. We are not privy to other family information. The image of Mary treasuring things in her heart (Luke 2:19, 51) gives insight to a mother's love when grownup children set out into the world on their own journey of life and faith that takes them beyond the close family ties.

MARY AT THE CROSS

Mary mother of James and Joses/Joseph appears among the women at the cross in Matthew and Mark. It is possible that this is a means of including Jesus' mother in the scene and indicating James and Joses/Joseph as brothers or close relatives of Jesus (Matt 27:56; Mark 15:40).

In John's Gospel, once again Mary is not named but simply called "the mother of Jesus" as she stands with other women and the "disciple whom he loved". Her role as mother is critical for John's theology. Jesus' words to his mother and this beloved disciple establish a new relationship between them as that between a mother and a son: "Woman, behold your son" (John 19:26*) and "Behold your mother" (John 19:27*). Responding to these words, "the disciple took her **as his own**" (19:27* — the Greek text does not indicate that the beloved disciple took her into his home, as is the long held tradition). In becoming "son" to the mother of

Jesus, the disciple now has a new relationship with Jesus (brother/sister) and a new relationship with God (son/child). In the resurrection account, Mary Magdalene is commissioned, "Go to my **brothers and sisters** and say to them, 'I am ascending to my father and **your Father**" (20:17). Although never named in this Gospel, the mother of Jesus has a key theological role enabling the evangelist to depict his theology as promised from the Prologue, "But to all who received him, who believed in his name, he gave power to become children of God" (1:12).

MARY AND THE RESURRECTION AND BEYOND

Luke includes Mary the mother of James among the women who announce the resurrection to the apostles (Luke 24:10). If, as above, she is Mary the mother of Jesus, then she is also witness to the resurrection.

At the beginning of Acts, believed to be the second volume attributed to Luke, Mary the mother of Jesus is included with all those gathered together and praying in Jerusalem after the ascension and awaiting the Holy Spirit (Acts 1:13–14). When Pentecost comes they are all gathered in the room so presumably Mary is with them. In Eastern icons Mary is depicted as central to the image, with the Holy Spirit above her. She stands out in her blue/purple robe with the apostles around her in plain coloured robes.

> When they had entered the city, they went to the room upstairs where they were staying, Peter, and John, and James, and Andrew, Philip and Thomas, Bartholomew and Matthew, James son of Alphaeus, and Simon the Zealot, and Judas son of James. ¹⁴ All these were constantly devoting themselves to prayer, together with certain women, **including Mary the mother of Jesus**, as well as his brothers.
> (Acts 1:13–14)

MARY THE MOTHER OF JESUS AND OUR MOTHER

In examining the scriptures we are able to revisit what we know of Mary in the New Testament. We know very little. Mary has few words to say. Her presence is powerful even in silence. She is the one who said yes to God to give birth to Jesus and in doing so gave birth to the Word of God active in the world. The later tradition adds to our understanding of Mary. She is our Mother as we are brothers and sisters of Jesus. She is our sister in discipleship and our model and inspiration in faithful service.

Below: Japanese image of Mary at Basilica of the Annunciation, Nazareth

DID YOU KNOW?

✠ Inside the Basilica of the Annunciation in Nazareth is the chapel of Mary believed to be at the site of the annunciation. Silence is maintained down in this chapel where people spend time in prayer. In the Basilica above mass is celebrated regularly and around the walls and outside in the courtyard are depictions of Mary from around the world, including Australia.

Mary Magdalene
Mary a Woman of Magdala

Mary Magdalene takes her name from the place she lived, Magdala (meaning tower in Aramaic). Today the modern town of Migdal (meaning tower in Hebrew) is close to the ancient site of Magdala. From the Sea of Galilee the location is marked by the cliffs of Arbel with Magdala lying below, a fishing port of the first century. From Magdala the ancient road wound through the valley around the cliffs to Cana, Nazareth and Sepphoris. Magdala is not recorded by name in the gospels as one of the places Jesus visited. It is possibly one of the towns Jesus and the disciples at least passed through in their ministry in Galilee. Excavation continues at the site today and includes the discovery of a first century CE synagogue.

First Witness to the Resurrection

Mary Magdalene is the first witness of the resurrection and sometimes referred to as "apostle". She is recorded in all four canonical gospels as witness to the resurrection and in Mark, Matthew and John as being at the crucifixion. Luke does not name her among the women who came with Jesus from Galilee, who looked on from a distance (Matt 27:55–56; Mark 15:40) or as in John, as one who stood near the cross (John 19:25). It is possible to assume Luke included her in the group, but his focus was on other characters at this time, especially the "good thief".

The suggestion of Mary Magdalene as apostle comes from her witness of the resurrection. Paul's claim to apostleship centred on two requirements: being witness to an appearance of the risen Christ and a divine call or commissioning to

Mary Magdalene icon

proclaim the good news of Christ.[2] Paul's experience on the road to Damascus fulfilled these two aspects and gave him confidence to align himself with the Twelve. Mary Magdalene has a significant relationship with Jesus, is witness to the resurrection and is recorded as encountering the risen Christ (John 20:12–18). There is ambiguity about whether she is commissioned, yet she is known as "apostle to the apostles", especially for her announcement of the resurrection to the apostles. This title comes to her in the third century via Hippolytus bishop and martyr of Rome. Pope Francis honoured her in 2016, reaffirming her status as "apostle to the apostles" and granting her a Saints Day in the calendar, giving honour to her witness.

Who is Mary Magdalene?

There is little known of Mary Magdalene. Her name is mentioned twelve times in the gospels in the New Testament. Her presence is mentioned in eleven of the twelve instances at the end of Jesus' ministry. Had Mary of Magdala been with Jesus and his followers throughout his ministry? She appears as though from the shadows into the spotlight in the crucial final scenes of Jesus' life, death and resurrection. Both Mark and Matthew give her pride of place among the women nearby at the crucifixion (Matt 27:55–56; Mark 15:40). Only Luke introduces her early in his narrative as being with Jesus and the Twelve as they set out proclaiming the good news (Luke 8:1–2). Luke mentions Mary Magdalene by name as having been healed of seven demons. It is her healing by Jesus that is important here. Because of this, she is following Jesus and is significant enough in the group to be named. Having made this inclusion, Luke does not make note of Mary Magdalene specifically when he recalls that there were women who had accompanied Jesus from Galilee who observed where his body was laid (Luke 23:55). Luke names her again and puts her in the first place among the women who tell the apostles of the resurrection. John includes Mary Magdalene with the mother of Jesus, her sister and Mary the wife of Clopas as he sets up his narrative for the new family Jesus will form from the cross through his mother and the beloved disciple (John 19:25). John then gives Mary Magdalene the sole role of witness to the resurrection and relates her personal encounter with the risen Jesus in the garden.

In this scene, the reader is brought into the intimacy of the moment and a glimpse of the deep love of Mary for Jesus and that of Jesus for her. She recognises Jesus when he calls her by name. She immediately responds, "Rabbouni" (teacher). Mary Magdalene is his disciple, a learner of this teacher. As she turns to him, we imagine that she goes to embrace him, and he warns her off, explaining that he has not yet ascended to the Father (John 20:17). He sends her to announce his resurrection to the disciples, now called brothers and sisters, which she does: "I have seen the Lord" (John 20:18). Mary Magdalene has come to a fullness of faith in the recognition of Jesus; she no longer calls him "teacher" but rather "Lord". She has come to believe.

DISPELLING THE MYTHS

Mary Magdalene has been incorrectly associated with the woman who anoints Jesus' feet in the Gospel of Luke (Luke 7:36–50). This account

> "…she turned around and saw Jesus standing there, but she did not know that it was Jesus. Jesus said to her, "Woman, why are you weeping? Whom are you looking for?" Supposing him to be the gardener, she said to him, "Sir, if you have carried him away, tell me where you have laid him, and I will take him away." Jesus said to her, "Mary!" She turned and said to him in Hebrew, "Rabbouni!" (which means Teacher).
>
> JOHN 20:14–16

Above: Noli me Tangere— Mary Magdalene greets the risen Christ

begins: "And a woman in the city, who was a sinner, having learned that he [Jesus] was eating in the Pharisee's house, brought an alabaster jar of ointment" (Luke 7:37). This woman is unnamed, as is the city. This is characteristic of Luke's scenarios, which allow his community members and readers through the ages to identify with the characters and to encounter Jesus. Nowhere in the New Testament is Mary Magdalene named as a sinner.

Mary Magdalene has also been mistaken for the woman caught in adultery in the Gospel of John (John 7:53–8:11). This scene begins with Jesus teaching in the Temple and the narrative tells us: "The scribes and the Pharisees brought a woman who had been caught in adultery" (John 8:3). Again there is no name given to this woman, and Mary Magdalene does not appear in this episode.

Only in Luke is Mary Magdalene reported as the one "from whom seven demons had gone out" (Luke 8:2). This phrase also appears in Mark 16:9; however, most scholars understand Mark's Gospel to end at 16:8, so this addition is likely to have come from a source common to Luke. This detail, not recorded by other evangelists, would indicate that Mary Magdalene was one of the women Jesus cured. If correct, it would give further reason for her faithfulness.

Mary Magdalene's prominence in the passion and her witness to the resurrection indicate she was a leader in the community of followers of Jesus. We can wonder about the leadership tensions that ensued over the early years of the development of the Jesus movement as communities endeavoured to live out the gospel, with its countercultural message, in the context of the Greco-Roman world.

Below: Sea of Galilee

> ### DID YOU KNOW?
>
> ✢ The story of Jesus' passion, death and resurrection was likely transmitted orally from the time of the events and through the early post-resurrection years. By the end of the first century CE, these events are recorded in all four gospels. These four accounts show a high degree of sequence of events, but they differ substantially in content. The differences give insight to the particular evangelist and the community for which it was written.

ELIZABETH

MOTHER OF JOHN THE BAPTIST AND MARY'S KINSWOMAN

Elizabeth, mother of John the Baptist and kinswoman of Mary, mother of Jesus, appears only in Luke's Gospel. The annunciation and birth of John the Baptist runs in parallel to that of the annunciation and birth of Jesus. Again we note that these narratives are more theology than history, so we pay attention to the symbols and how the characters indicate Luke's theology of Jesus coming to the poor, the "little ones" and the outsiders.

Elizabeth is introduced with reference to her husband Zechariah: "his wife was a descendent of Aaron, and her name was Elizabeth" (Luke 1:5). While Zechariah offers incense in the sanctuary of the Temple according to his priestly duty, the angel Gabriel appears to him and announces:

> "Do not be afraid, Zechariah, for your prayer has been heard. Your wife Elizabeth will bear you a son, and you will name him John. You will have joy and gladness, and many will rejoice at his birth, for he will be great in the sight of the Lord. He must never drink wine or strong drink; even before his birth he will be filled with the Holy Spirit. He will turn many of the people of Israel to the Lord their God. With the spirit and power of Elijah he will go before him, to turn the hearts of parents to their children, and the disobedient to the wisdom of the righteous, to make ready a people prepared for the Lord." (Luke 1:13–17)

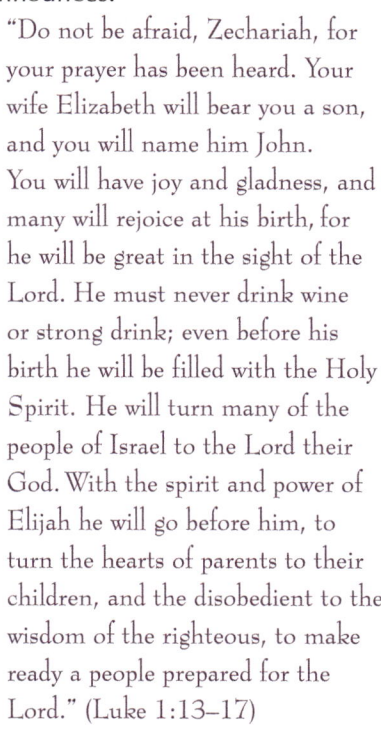

Right: Sculpture of Elizabeth and Mary, En Kerem

Zechariah questions the announcement, and Gabriel strikes him mute for his unbelief. The people praying outside work out that he must have seen a vision when Zechariah cannot speak to them. But what of Elizabeth? Her husband returns mute; she knows nothing of the vision or the message of Gabriel. She conceives and as a woman of faith says, "This is what the Lord has done for me when he looked favourably on me and took away the disgrace I have endured among my people" (Luke 1:25). Elizabeth echoes the memory of Hannah in 1 Samuel, who also had no children and pleaded in prayer to God for a male child whom she vowed to devote to the Lord. Elizabeth also had borne the shame of not bearing any children, and she is described as "barren".

Yet Elizabeth and Zechariah are described as "righteous before God, living blamelessly according to all the commandments and regulations of the Lord" (Luke 1:6). Their background shows their perseverance and fidelity over many years. They echo the Old Testament faithfulness to God and of God.

Compare the revelation of Gabriel in the book of Daniel with those to Zechariah and Mary. See how familiar the words are and how Luke has drawn on them to shape his birth narrative.

Dan 7:16	I approached one who stood in the presence of God*
Dan 8:17	and when he came, I became frightened
Dan 9:21	while I was speaking in prayer, the man Gabriel … came to me in swift flight at the time of the evening sacrifice.
Dan 9:23	for you are greatly beloved.
Dan 10:11	I have now been sent to you.
Dan 10:12	He said to me, "Do not fear, Daniel …"
Dan 10:15	I turned my face toward the ground and was speechless.
Dan 10:16	Then … I opened my mouth to speak, and said
Dan 7:28	but I kept all these things in my heart*

"BLESSED ARE YOU AMONG WOMEN AND BLESSED IS THE FRUIT OF YOUR WOMB"

LUKE 1:42

"WHEN ELIZABETH HEARD MARY'S GREETING,
THE CHILD LEAPED IN HER WOMB.
AND ELIZABETH WAS FILLED WITH HOLY SPIRIT"

LUKE 1:41

THE VISITATION – MARY AND ELIZABETH

The narrator notes a six month time gap and introduces the coming of angel Gabriel to Nazareth for the annunciation of Jesus' birth to Mary. At the end of this episode, the angel Gabriel advises Mary of the news of Elizabeth's pregnancy. This is the imperative that moves Mary to visit her kinswoman in the sixth month and stay to assist with the birth of her baby (Luke 1:39–40).

Elizabeth recognises Mary as "mother of my Lord" and proclaims, "Blessed are you among women and blessed is the fruit of your womb" (Luke 1:42). The joyful greeting and loving embrace of these two faithful kinswomen gives us in one moment a view of their loving care for one another and a cameo of their openness to God. These two women, old and young, symbolically bring God's promise from the Old Testament and the fulfilment of that promise in the New Testament together in joyful embrace. Elizabeth and Mary are willing collaborators in the initiative of God and bringing to birth the herald, John the Baptist, and the Word made flesh, Jesus.

In many ways Elizabeth is overshadowed by the recounting of the story of Zechariah her husband and the birth of John the Baptist. Elizabeth holds her place here as a named woman with at least as strong a lineage as her husband and kinswoman of Mary. She is remembered for her role in salvation history. She, along with Mary and Anna, sets the stage in Luke's Gospel for God's reversal of world values, focusing on the story of Jesus and the least important people in society.

Elizabeth did not give up on God even though her own life situation had caused her pain and shame. Her faithfulness is inspirational today for women whose dreams are unfulfilled. Her praise of Mary and their journey together in their pregnancies offer a model of kinship, friendship and support in accepting the call of God and living out their part in building the reign of God.

ANNA

HANNAH IN HEBREW, HANNA IN GREEK

We encounter Anna only in Luke's Gospel and find her in the Temple as an old woman. She appears at the time Jesus' parents came for their purification and to present Jesus to the Lord. In the usual Lukan pairing pattern of male and female, the scene is constructed with Simeon and Anna, also paralleling Zechariah and Elizabeth. Jesus is first taken up by Simeon "to do what was customary under the law" (Luke 2:27). After Simeon's praise of God and predictions for Jesus and his mother, Anna is introduced. In just three short verses we are given a snapshot of her. Anna by her name also recalls Hannah from 1 Samuel (see 1 Sam 1:2–22; 2:1, 21), whose pleading prayers to God for a male child are answered and who devotes Samuel to the Lord. As a prophet she also recalls a woman prophet, Huldah (2 Kgs 22:14–20), who is called to read the scrolls found in the floor of the Temple. Anna is a childless widow who has devoted most of her life to worshipping in the Temple (see also the section on widows). She is the poorest of the poor, with no husband

> There was also a prophet, Anna the daughter of Phanuel, of the tribe of Asher. She was of a great age, having lived with her husband seven years after her marriage, then as a widow to the age of eighty-four. She never left the temple but worshiped there with fasting and prayer night and day. At that moment she came, and began to praise God and to speak about the child to all who were looking for the redemption of Jerusalem.
> LUKE 2:36–38

and no son, bereft of social and economic support. Yet she has the privilege to greet the Messiah. The references to Phanuel and the tribe of Asher indicate her possible closeness to Jerusalem and her longing for the coming of the Messiah, a long held hope of Simeon as well. Anna is steeped in the Hebrew Scriptures, and her faithfulness gives her sight to recognise Jesus as the Messiah. Anna proclaims Jesus "to all who were looking for the redemption of Jerusalem" (Luke 2:18).

Anna, widowed without children, may have had little option for survival other than the Temple where widows would be cared for. The connections to the Old Testament women assist us to imagine her prayers over those long years. As a prophet, she reminds women today of their prophetic role. The contribution that Anna makes by her presence, her prayer and the wisdom she imparts in her later years reminds us of the dignity, worth and contribution of older people today.

Below: Spindle whorls and spindles, Jordan Museum, Amman, Jordan

JOANNA

Joanna makes her appearance in a summary passage (Luke 8:1–3) announcing that Jesus is heading out on his journey "proclaiming the good news of the kingdom of God" (Luke 8:1). He sets out accompanied by the twelve and some women who "had been cured of evil spirits and infirmities" (Luke 8:3). Joanna is named along with Mary Magdalene and Susanna even though there are many more "who provided for them out of their resources". So Joanna is significant as one of the women disciples accompanying Jesus. Joanna is further identified as the wife of Chuza, Herod's steward. Herod set up his palace in Tiberius, and Chuza is named as Herod's steward. Joanna, along with her husband, are likely members of the Herodian household and may have been among those impelled to take up residence in the new capital. It is not clear how Joanna can be away from her husband on the mission of Jesus. Perhaps she left her husband and took her dowry with her. Perhaps she accompanied the mission for periods of time in the Galilee region and her husband was tolerant of her absences.

Along the way, Joanna does not feature by name again until the resurrection (Luke 24:10). Did she travel to Jerusalem for the feasts and accompany Jesus and his followers there? Luke's narrative relates: "The women who had come with him from Galilee followed, and they saw the tomb and how his body was laid" (Luke 23:55). It was "they" who came to the tomb on the first day of the week (Luke 24:1), who found the stone rolled away (Luke 24:2) and who found no body (Luke 24:3). It was also "they" who were frightened by the men in dazzling

DID YOU KNOW?

✠ Herod Antipas, son of Herod the Great, ruled Galilee and Perea as Tetrarch 4BCE – 39 CE and established Tiberius as the capital where he built a palace. Historian Flavius Josephus (Antiquities of the Jews 18.36–38) tells us of this foundation:

And now Herod the tetrarch, who was in great favour with Tiberius, built a city of the same name with him, and called it Tiberias. He built it in the best part of Galilee, at the lake of Gennesareth. There are warm baths at a little distance from it, in a village named Emmaus. Strangers came and inhabited this city; a great number of the inhabitants were Galileans also; and many were necessitated by Herod to come thither out of the country belonging to him, and were by force compelled to be its inhabitants; some of them were persons of condition. He also admitted poor people, such as those that were collected from all parts, to dwell in it. Some of them were not quite free, and these he was benefactor to, and made them free in great numbers; but obliged them not to forsake the city, by building them very good houses at his own expenses, and by giving them land also; for he was sensible, that to make this place a habitation was to transgress the Jewish ancient laws, because many sepulchres were to be here taken away, in order to make room for the city Tiberias whereas our laws pronounce that such inhabitants are unclean for seven days.

robes who reminded them about what Jesus had told them, and it was "they who remembered" (Luke 24:8) and went to tell the rest. "They" had accompanied Jesus, witnessed his proclamation and now they themselves brought the good news. In Luke 24:10 it is revealed that Joanna is one of the "they", along with Mary Magdalene and Mary the mother of James, as well as the other women with them. Joanna has journeyed from the beginning in faith, accompanying Jesus, witnessing his proclamation of the good news and continuing to provide for him and the disciples. Here Joanna is one who is still providing, bringing spices to anoint his body and finding that what Jesus had told them was true. Joanna is one who is witness to the resurrection and tells the good news to the apostles.

There is some suggestion that Johanna is one and the same as Junia (see page 38), having taken on a Roman name that sounds like her own. This assumption also requires her husband Chuza to have taken on the name "Andronicus". While possible, this is a stretch of the imagination in light of little evidence.

Joanna is a woman in the inner circle of those accompanying Jesus and recorded in Luke. She is remembered as a witness to the empty tomb and for announcing the resurrection of Jesus to the disciples along with Mary Magdalene and Mary the mother of James.

> NOW IT WAS MARY MAGDALENE, JOANNA, MARY THE MOTHER OF JAMES, AND THE OTHER WOMEN WITH THEM WHO TOLD THIS TO THE APOSTLES.
>
> LUKE 24:10

SUSANNA

Susanna is named with Mary Magdalene and Joanna, wife of Chuza, as one of the women, among many, who had been healed of evil spirits or infirmities and who provided for Jesus and his apostles and the whole entourage out of their resources (Luke 8:3). This is Susanna's only appearance. She may have still been with the women who had followed Jesus from Galilee, who stood at a distance when Jesus died on the cross (Luke 23:49), and she may have gone to the tomb with the women early on the first day of the week, but she is not named with Mary Magdalene and Joanna as announcing the resurrection to the apostles. Her omission may mean that she was not attested as witness to this event and so not named.

Susanna holds her place of honour in being named as one who accompanied Jesus as he proclaimed the good news. She was restored to community through healing by Jesus and became one of his followers, eager for the mission and on the journey. Susanna reminds women today of their changing roles through life, sometimes in the limelight and at other times dedicated to the ordinary demands, struggles and joys of the journey of life.

Mary the Mother of James
and Joses/Joseph

At the death of Jesus Mary the mother of James the younger (literally "little") and of Joses is named along with Mary Magdalene, Salome and other women who were looking on at a distance (Mark 15:40). As the scene advances, she is referred to as Mary of Joses (Mark 15:47) and Mary of James (Mark 16:1). Having been described in 15:40 as the mother, it is clear in the other instances of "of Joses" and "of James" that the relationship is of mother to son.

Earlier in Mark's Gospel, in recounting the rejection of Jesus in Nazareth, his hometown, those in the synagogue where he taught on the Sabbath asked, "Is not this the carpenter, the son of Mary and brother of James and Joses and Judas and Simon, and are not his sisters here with us?" (Mark 6:3). This would indicate that Mary mother of James and Joses is a relative of Jesus and James and Joses are his cousins. The term "brother" can include close kinship relations, not necessarily indicating a child of the same mother.

In Matthew's account, Mary the mother of James and Joseph is named along with Mary Magdalene and the mother of the sons of Zebedee, who are among the women standing at a distance from the crucifixion, who

> Meanwhile, standing near the cross of Jesus were his mother, and his mother's sister, Mary the wife of Clopas, and Mary Magdalene.
> John 19:25

have followed Jesus from Galilee and provided for him. At the burial it is Mary Magdalene and "the other Mary" who are sitting opposite the tomb (Matt 28:1). Presumably this is Mary the mother of James and Joseph.

Luke names Mary mother of James (literally Mary of James) with Mary Magdalene and Joanna as the ones who announce the resurrection to the apostles (Luke 24:10). Mary's relationship with James is not explicitly indicated as mother, but the expression "Mary of James" is used for mother and son where this is the relationship known to the community. She is not included by name by Luke in 8:2–3 among the women who accompany Jesus in his ministry.

In John's Gospel, Mary of Clopas stands near the cross of Jesus and Mary the mother of James and Joses is not named. Some suggest Mary of Clopas may be the mother of James and Joses. Significant work by Richard Bauckham offers evidence to the contrary (see Mary of Clopas below).[3]

The distance of time and place for present day readers creates a disadvantage. The communities addressed by Mark, Matthew, Luke and John likely understood exactly who Mary the mother of James was. Even today a person can have a number of titles by which they are known in relation to family members and in various communities. Mary the mother of James and Joses features as one of the witnesses to Jesus' death and resurrection and is one of the significant women who travelled with and provided for Jesus during his ministry.

Mary of Clopas

Mary the wife of Clopas (literally Mary of Clopas) is named by John as standing near the cross in the company of other women. What is not immediately clear is whether there are four or three women. Bauckham investigated the possibilities and deduced that Mary of Clopas is Jesus' aunt (his mother's sister).[4] He does not stop there but investigates the relationship of Mary to Clopas. The options would be that he is her father, her husband or her son. Examining the use of the terminology used in the New Testament and epigraphical evidence from Jewish Palestine, Bauckham determines that Mary was probably the wife or unmarried daughter of Clopas.[5] To solve the issue, the investigation turned to identifying Clopas. This proved not to be very difficult, as it is detailed by Hegesippus, a second century writer, that the successor to James the Lord's brother as head of the Jerusalem church was Simon (or Symeon), the son of Clopas.[6] Clopas was the brother of Joseph, who was betrothed to Mary. Mary is then wife of Clopas and sister-in-law to Mary the mother of Jesus.

From this deduction, Mary wife of Clopas is mother of Simon (Symeon), not James and Joses. Her inclusion here indicates her significance in the community of John. The spotlight falls on another woman linked closely with Jesus by familial links and in company with Mary Magdalene.

MARTHA AND MARY

Martha and Mary appear in both the gospels of Luke and John (Luke 10:38–42; John 11:17–44; 12:1–8). They are sisters and followers of Jesus. Their inclusion is intriguing. Many have expected to discover insights into the ministry of women with Jesus through them, yet the narratives are ambiguous, leaving much to the imagination. They do appear to have a close relationship with Jesus and, in the Johannine tradition, Jesus is friend of the family and a regular visitor to their house.

LUKAN CAMEO OF MARTHA AND MARY

Martha and Mary first appear in a story related by Luke. This is a little cameo exemplary story where the characters are less important than their actions, so we learn little about the two women. In Luke's narrative, Jesus entered a "certain village" (Luke 10:38). Here in this unnamed village "a woman named Martha" (Luke 10:38) welcomed Jesus into her home. As Martha is the one inviting Jesus in, she may be head of household. Her welcoming holds the meaning of entertaining a guest and offering hospitality. There is no indication that he knew her but as the story unfolds, both Martha and her sister appear to be disciples. Martha's sister is Mary, who, we are informed, "sat at the Lord's feet listening to what he was saying" (Luke 10:39). Martha busies herself, "distracted by many tasks" (Luke 10:40). The word for "tasks" is *diakonia,* which conveys serving at table as well as ministry. The double meaning is likely, giving Luke the opportunity to teach at more than one level. Martha then comes to Jesus to ask, "Lord, do you not care that my sister has left me to do all the work by myself? Tell her then to help me" (Luke 10:40). Is this sibling rivalry? Should Mary indeed have helped her sister, whose "many tasks" are likely concerned with offering hospitality? Her help would have meant that they might both sit down together and listen to Jesus. Does this also allude to the ministry of women and the limitations? Jesus' answer comes as a surprise, "Martha, Martha, you are

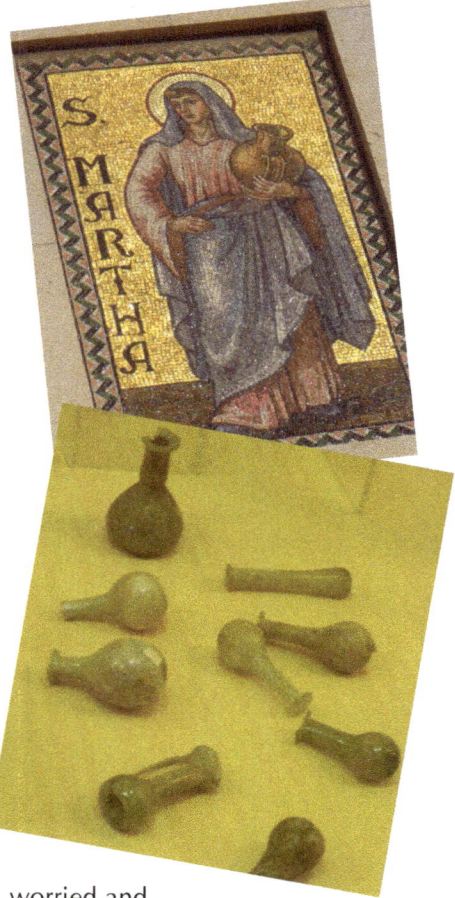

worried and distracted by many things: there is need of only one thing. Mary has chosen the better part, which will not be taken away from her" (Luke 10:41). Jesus' affirmation of the place of the silent Mary accords with other instances of Luke's depictions limiting the roles of women. This passage lies between the Good Samaritan and Jesus teaching the disciples to pray. This exemplary tale may also be the glue to show the tension between good works and prayer. There are many perspectives on this passage, but let us not be distracted from these two sisters: Martha and Mary. They are living out their life of faith in the best way that they can, and they teach us about considering balance in our lives, taking time out to listen and be with Jesus and giving priority to his presence in our lives. Martha reminds us that the tasks of hospitality and ministry are demanding, but Jesus does not let that be an excuse.

MEETING MARY AND MARTHA IN JOHN'S GOSPEL

The Gospel of John introduces these two sisters in the reverse order: "Now a certain man was ill, Lazarus of Bethany, the village of Mary and her sister Martha" (John 11:1). Mary and Martha are identified as being of the village of Bethany. John's Gospel identifies Mary as "the one who anointed the Lord with perfume/ointment and wiped his feet with her hair" (John 11:2; see also Luke 7:36–50 and "Woman who anointed Jesus" in this volume, page 24). In the same verse Lazarus is revealed as her brother, making Mary, Martha and Lazarus siblings. The sisters send a message to Jesus: "Lord, he whom you love is ill" (John 11:3). The narrator advises: "Jesus loved Martha and her sister and Lazarus" (John 11:5).

Yet he did not come immediately and when he arrived, Lazarus was already in the tomb for four days (John 11:17). Hearing that Jesus was coming, Martha went out to meet him and Mary stayed at home. Martha's encounter with Jesus sets up the occasion for her to declare her faith and for Jesus to acclaim, "I am the resurrection and the life, those who believe in me even though they die, will live, and everyone who lives and believes in me will never die" (John 11:25). In response, Martha expresses perfect faith in Jesus: "Yes, Lord, I believe that you are the Messiah, the Son of God, the one coming into the world" (John 11:27). In the Synoptic Gospels, it is Peter who makes this first declaration of faith. Martha's words are repeated by the evangelist at the conclusion of the Gospel to indicate her faith is the ultimate goal of this Gospel: "But these are written so that you may come to believe that Jesus is the Messiah, the Son of God, and that through believing you may have life in his name" (John 20:31). In the raising of Lazarus, Martha's faith takes central place. Mary's faith is expressed in the following chapter.

John's Gospel returns to Bethany and the house of Lazarus in 12:1–8, where Jesus is at dinner with them.

> "Yes, Lord, I believe that you are the Messiah, the Son of God, the one coming into the world."
> JOHN 11:27

Martha serves (*diakoneō*) and Lazarus is at table with Jesus while Mary anoints his feet with pure nard and wipes them with her hair. Here John's account recalls the story of a woman who anointed Jesus' feet before his passion. Both Mark and Matthew record such a memory, as is noted in the next section. Mary's action of anointing the feet of Jesus will be replicated by Jesus in the next chapter when he washes the feet of his disciples. Mary's loving service to Jesus becomes the model Jesus teaches his disciples: "So if I, your Lord and Teacher, have washed your feet, you also ought to wash one another's feet" (John 13:14).

Left: Icon of St Martha from Church of Lazarus, Bethany, Israel
Left below: Perfume bottles
Below: Jesus, Martha and Mary from the Church of St Francis Xavier, Malacca, Malaysia

WOMAN WHO ANOINTED JESUS

There are three different versions in the four gospels of the anointing of Jesus by a woman (Mark 14:3–9; Matt 26:6–13; Luke 7:36–50; John 12:1–8). In Mark and Matthew, the narrative relates the story of an unnamed woman who anoints Jesus' head at the beginning of the passion narrative. In Luke, it is a different story and occurs earlier in the narrative. The woman is identified as a sinner who first washes Jesus' feet with her tears and wipes them with her hair before anointing them with oil. In John's account, the woman is named as Mary, sister of Martha and Lazarus, who anoints Jesus' feet prior to his passion (see section on Martha and Mary).

IN MEMORY OF HER

Mark "sandwiches" the story of the woman who anoints Jesus within the narrative of his betrayal. In this way, he focuses the light on the woman, contrasting to the shadows of the treachery and betrayal. This woman recognises who Jesus is and treats him accordingly. Her "good deed" will be told in memory of her whenever the good news is proclaimed in the whole world (Mark 14:9).

The event is set two days before Passover and the feast of the unleaven bread. Jesus is in the house of Simon the leper at Bethany, reclining for a meal, when a woman comes in with an expensive alabaster jar of nard, breaks it open, and pours it on the head of Jesus (Mark 14:3). The aromatic, luxurious perfume of the nard would have pervaded the room. The woman's gesture reflects the anointing of kings, such as Samuel's anointing of Saul (1 Sam 10:1) and David (1 Sam 16:13) as well as Nathan's anointing of Solomon (1 Kgs 1:34–40). She acts as prophet, revealing Jesus as Messiah (in Greek *christos* = anointed) and messianic king. In the midst of disciples, she alone recognises who Jesus is and anoints his head.

Her action provoked indignation about the wastefulness of lavishing this ointment on Jesus. He defends her action, calling it a "good deed" (14:6). In this way, he reinterprets her action as an act of mercy and deflects the messianic focus to point to his death and ultimately to his resurrection. Her "good deed" will be told in memory of her whenever the good news is proclaimed in the whole world (Mark 14:9). Ironically, her name is not recorded or remembered but the betrayer's is.

The woman who anoints Jesus is pivotal to the faith of disciples. At the moment when the narrative moves toward the death of Jesus, she is the light of memory beyond the death to the resurrection and the proclamation of the good news. Otherwise, all we are left with is an empty tomb and women who have fled in terror and amazement for they were afraid. The prophetic action of the woman in Mark has a dramatic and significant place in his narrative. This cameo of an unnamed woman adds to a number of instances where the presence and action of women who followed and accompanied Jesus was significant enough to be remembered in the gospels.

Matthew's account follows Mark's closely. Matthew redeems the women at the tomb, saying that they left the tomb with fear *and great joy* and were going to tell his disciples. Matthew's account still preserves the prophetic act of the woman who anoints Jesus yet he adds an appearance of Jesus, to the women at the tomb and has

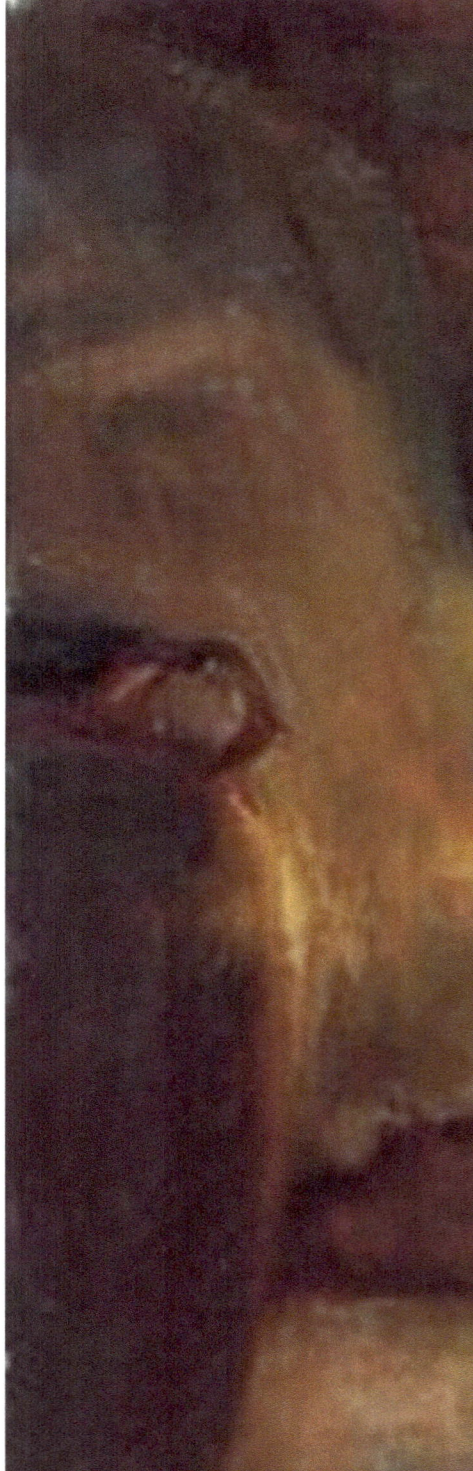

Right: Woman anointing Jesus' feet

them worship him in the same way as all those who have recognised Jesus through Matthew's Gospel. His "brothers" will also "see" him if they follow the instruction of the women. Matthew ensures that his Gospel ends with the command of Jesus that they "go therefore and make disciples of all nations…". In his teaching style, Matthew coaches his community in their discipleship.

THE LUKAN ANOINTING: LOVE AND THANKFULNESS

The woman who anoints Jesus in Luke seems to be a completely different story and a different woman. In Luke 7:36–50, the woman is a sinner. She washes Jesus' feet with her tears and wipes them dry with her hair before anointing them. Hers is a demonstration of love, for she has been forgiven: "Therefore, I tell you, her sins, which were many, have been forgiven; hence she has shown great love. But the one to whom little is forgiven, loves little" (Luke 7:47). The anointing occurs in a series of actions centring on Jesus' feet. She is not performing an act of mercy, preparing for his death or proclaiming him as messiah. Her action shows the proper response to Jesus in contrast to Simon the Pharisee.

A WOMAN HEALED AND A DAUGHTER RESTORED TO LIFE

These two unnamed women are inextricably linked in the Synoptic Gospels. The story of the raising of the twelve-year-old girl is interposed with the story of the woman suffering twelve years from haemorrhaging. Jesus addresses the woman as "daughter", giving her a familial link and a belonging where she had none, in contrast to the daughter of the synagogue official who is clearly part of a family and community. The woman acts on her own behalf and it is Jairus/Synagogue Official who entreats Jesus' assistance for his daughter.

SAVED AND HEALED THROUGH FAITH ACCORDING TO MARK

Mark's account is the longest version. The woman emerges from among "the large crowd: pressing in on Jesus as he follows Jairus the synagogue leader to where his daughter lays ill in his house (Mark 6:25). The crowd is likely made up of many people with hopes of healing, some curious about this man Jesus, some who have come with family and friends expecting to hear him and see his miraculous deeds. This woman does not appear to stand out among the crowd. She is able to get close to Jesus, and it is her faith that becomes her identifying characteristic. She has no advocate like the daughter of Jairus. She is not named and has no status, no importance. She has suffered much (Mark 5:26), which is expressed by the same Greek verb

Below: Sarcophagus of the Mourning Women of Sidon, 4th century BCE, Istanbul Archaeological Museum, Turkey

as describes Jesus' suffering and fate (Mark 8:31). When she came up behind him in the crowd, she only wanted to touch his *himation*, a garment-like a cloak that was wrapped around over his tunic. She did not want to touch his body or want him to touch her or to even realise her presence. The narrator offers us her words: "If I but touch his clothes, I will be saved" (Mark 8:28). In each of the tellings of this story, the evangelists use the verb *sōzō*, which means to save or rescue and can be used for being healed or recovering from illness. It seems to be inadequate to leave this faith story connected to healing of the illness alone. For Mark, the double meaning is not only possible but probable.

Twice in succession, events take place "immediately". Firstly she immediately becomes aware in her body that she has been healed of her affliction (Mark 5:29). Secondly, Jesus is immediately aware that power has gone out of him and he asks, "Who touched my clothes?" (Mark 5:30). The disciples miss the nuance and bluntly retort about how he could say "who touched me" in such a pressing crowd. With Jesus looking around, the woman owns up, falling on her knees before him, trembling in fear (Mark 5:33). It is at that moment that Jesus calls her "Daughter" and speaks of her faith saving her; he bids her to "go in peace, and be healed of your disease". The episode ends on this note as news comes from Jairus' household. She is acclaimed for her faith, saved and healed.

> He said to her,
> "Daughter, your faith has saved you;*
> go in peace,
> and be healed of your disease."
> MARK 5:34

> JESUS TURNED, AND SEEING HER HE SAID,
> "TAKE HEART, DAUGHTER; YOUR FAITH HAS SAVED YOU."
> AND AT THAT HOUR THE WOMAN WAS SAVED.*
>
> MATT 9:22

HEALED THROUGH FAITH ACCORDING TO MATTHEW

Matthew's account reduces the story to just three verses. The woman appears suddenly behind Jesus as he and the disciples are following the synagogue leader to his house as his daughter has just died. There is no crowd pressing in so when the woman touches the fringe or border or tassel of his *himation* he turns around and immediately sees her, saying, "Take heart, daughter, your faith has made you well" (Matt 9:22). From that moment she was made well. The healing does not occur with her touching the fringe of his garment but with the word of Jesus. No power goes out from him without his word.

TRANSFORMED BY FAITH ACCORDING TO LUKE

In Luke's narrative, elements of both Mark's and Matthew's account are retained. The crowd is pressing around and she comes up behind Jesus and touches the fringe of his *himation*. On her touch she is cured and Jesus asks, "Who touched me?" Luke adds, "When all denied it" (Luke 8:45), before having Peter address Jesus as Master and exclaim about the crowd. The woman comes

Above: The healing of a bleeding woman, Catacombs of Marcellinus and Peter, Rome

forward and falls on her knees, trembling and declares in front of everyone why she touched Jesus and how she was healed immediately. It is then that Jesus addresses her, saying, "Daughter, your faith has made you well; go in peace" (Luke 8:48). Here the woman who was anonymous in the crowd becomes one who proclaims the good news that has happened to her, and she is acclaimed for her faith.

All three evangelists acclaim her for her faith and maintain the twelve years of suffering she endured. They also all insert this woman's story in the middle of one about the dead or dying twelve-year-old daughter of the synagogue leader.

A DAUGHTER RESTORED TO LIFE

Similarly, there are three versions of the raising of the twelve-year-old daughter of the synagogue leader, known as Jairus in Mark and Luke's versions. We know very little about her other than that she was dying or already dead. Jesus takes her by the hand in all three renditions, and in Mark and Luke, Jesus asks or calls to her to get up (Mark 5:41; Luke 8:54). Jesus does not lay his hands on her as he is requested in both Mark and Matthew. He takes her by the hand, leading her into life.

SAMARITAN WOMAN AT THE WELL

The Samaritan woman only appears in the Gospel according to John (John 4:7–42). She never reveals her name. As a Samaritan, she is connected to a particular place, community of people and history. She does not seek Jesus out but finds him at the well where she comes to draw water.

The Samaritan woman at the well exemplifies the journey of one who comes to believe. In chapter 20 the narrator tells us, "Now Jesus did many other signs in the presence of his disciples which are not written in this book. But these are written so that you may come to believe" (John 20:30–31). The story of the Samaritan woman comes within a group of stories about various people at various stages of becoming believers. This section begins with the exemplar of Mary having perfect faith (John 2:1–11) and ends with another such example, the royal official (John 4:46–54).[7]

AT JACOB'S WELL

The encounter of Jesus with the Samaritan woman occurs at Jacob's well on a plot of land that Jacob gave to Joseph, his son, at Sychar in Samaria. These details cement her religious context and identify a tension between them as Judean and Samaritan as well as tensions relating to their place of worship, Jerusalem or Gerizim respectively. Jesus has stopped there on his journey and the woman comes to draw water (John 4:7). The ensuing conversation crosses the divide of male and female, and of Judean and Samaritan, leading to a new possibility personally for the Samaritan woman and also generally for the end of division of worship.

> The Samaritan woman said to him,
> "How is it that you, a Judean, ask a drink of me, a woman of Samaria?"
> (Judeans do not share things in common with Samaritans.) *
> JOHN 4:9

A WOMAN AND A MAN – A SAMARITAN AND A JUDEAN

Jesus initiates the conversation. The disciples have gone to the city so this is a personal encounter. It is awkward being between a Judean and a Samaritan, a man and a woman. At the outset the woman is not open to what Jesus is speaking about.[3] They are not on the same wavelength. Jesus' offer of living water (John 4:14) is misunderstood by the woman, who at first sees it as a means of saving her coming to the well every day. Jesus goes in deeper to speak of her life and offers a resolution to the divide of worship between Jerusalem and Gerizim. She calls him "prophet" and begins to open her heart.

As the discussion moves into the level of belief, she speaks of the coming Messiah, and Jesus reveals who he is: he is the one. This is the moment of understanding. Here what she knows and believes to be true is revealed as happening in her presence.

> The woman said to him,
> "I know that Messiah is coming" (who is called Christ).
> "When he comes, he will proclaim all things to us."
> Jesus said to her,
> "I am he, the one who is speaking to you."
> JOHN 4:25–26

A SAMARITAN WOMAN CAME TO DRAW WATER, AND JESUS SAID TO HER, "GIVE ME A DRINK."
JOHN 4:7

DID YOU KNOW?

✢ There is a small group, between 500–700, of Samaritans who believe they are the remnant of the ancient Northern Kingdom of Israel, descendants of the tribes of Joseph, Menashe and Levi. They are about equally divided between Holon near Tel Aviv in Israel and Mt Gerizim near Nablus in Palestine. They call themselves "Bene- Yisrael Ha -Shamerem" which means "Keepers" or, more correctly, "Children of Israel". They observe the ancient Israelite tradition since the time of Moses. They have five principles of faith: one God, one prophet Moses, one Torah, the Pentateuch (first five books written by Moses), one holy place, Mt Gerizim, and Vengeance Day (the day when a prophet like Moses from the tribe of Joseph will come).

Right: From the Church of Santa Maria dei Servi, Padua, Italy by R. Czemesini (1988)

BELIEVING AND PROCLAIMING

The disciples return, and the focus moves from the woman, who leaves her water jar and returns to the city. Once there she engages the people: "Come and see a man who told me everything I have ever done! He cannot be the Messiah can he?" She is still processing what happened to her. They go and see based only on her word and later invite Jesus to stay with them, coming to believe on their own account. Even while on her own journey, she brings others to believe. Her journey will go on, and we will not know when or how she comes to full faith as the page turns on this episode and she disappears from the narrative.

The imagery of the woman at the well allows deep contemplation of the metaphors. In the midst of an ordinary task, she encounters Jesus and is invited to go deeper. While beginning in doubt, she does keep the conversation going, which leads ultimately to her recognising who Jesus is and her role of witness to her community. It is the continuing conversation that engages life and belief.

This encounter between the Samaritan woman and a Judean man symbolically points back to the reunification of the two kingdoms, as described in Ezekiel 37, where God can again dwell among them.[9] The Samaritans come to believe in Jesus as "Saviour of the world" (John 4:42), so bringing an end to division, because of the openness and coming to faith of the Samaritan woman along with her theological insight and witness.

THE SYROPHOENICIAN WOMAN AND THE CAANANITE WOMAN

This appears to be the same story told from the perspectives of two evangelists, Matthew and Mark, in a manner most relevant to the community to whom they are writing. In Matthew's Gospel, this is the first time a woman is given direct speech. She comes out of pagan territory and meets Jesus in a public space. This woman is a Canaanite, linking back to two other Canaanite women, Tamar and Rahab, mentioned in the genealogy in Matthew 1:3, 5. This Canaanite woman joins the other two in their ability to overcome reluctance or indecision of Jewish/Israelite men, acknowledge the priority of Israel in salvation and achieve their objectives through clever speech and action.

In the gospels of Mark and Matthew, the daughters of these women are the only women who are specifically noted to be possessed by demons. The other specific instances are men. In both gospels, the casting out of demons is one of the reasons the crowds flock to Jesus (Mark 1:32, 34, 39; Matt 4:24; 7:22, 8:16) and the chosen twelve are sent out to preach and cast out demons (Mark 3:14-15; Matt 10:8). In both these accounts, the focus is on the mother's faith. There is no interaction between Jesus and the daughter nor the demon.

SYROPHOENICIAN WOMAN

The Syrophoenician woman reveals a perspective of Jesus that is none too comfortable. Her request appears as reasonable as many, especially as it is healing for her daughter rather than herself. Her encounter with Jesus shows her recognition of him and her faith that he can heal. She pushes him to reconsider.

This woman is clearly demarcated as being in the region of Tyre; she is called "Syrophoenician" and Gentile. Jesus is not in the region to expand his mission to the Gentiles but to have some time out. So from the beginning we can understand her courage, faith and persistence in that immediately on hearing about him, she seeks out Jesus at the house where he is staying.[10] She comes, and falls prostrate at his feet (Mark 7:25). She begs that Jesus cast out the demon from her daughter (Mark 7:26). Jesus' response is offensive to her and to our ears. Why would he reject her plea? Earlier in Mark's narrative (Mark 5:1–20) Jesus has crossed to the other side of the Sea of Galilee, to the country of the Gerasenes, which was Gentile territory. Here, Jesus was confronted by a man with an unclean spirit, coming from the tombs. The Gerasene demoniac is healed. So we have seen Jesus expand his mission to the Gentiles. So why not to her? The Syrophoenician woman, like Jairus, is not asking healing for herself but for her daughter.

Despite Jesus' retort to her she argues back, "Sir, even the dogs under the table eat the children's crumbs" (Mark 7:28). Her response has Jesus change his mind as he says, "For saying that you may go – the demon has left your daughter" (Mark 7:29). Jesus does not compliment her faith, yet we can see that her faith has affected Jesus, and we are informed by the narrator that when she returned home she found her daughter lying on the bed and the demon had gone (Mark 7:30).

DID YOU KNOW?

✣ Explanation of the demons is often given in the modern context as mental illness. Yet it is important to appreciate the context of demons in the time of Jesus and the writing of the Gospels. From the beginning of each of the Synoptic Gospels (Matthew, Mark and Luke), Jesus is established as the Messiah, the Son of God. Through the miraculous healing and casting out of demons, it is evident that Jesus has power and authority over Satan and sin and ushers in the reign of God. The Gospel writers are not engaged in describing the myths and superstitions of demonologies of the time but rather confirming the identity of Jesus, who even the demons recognise; for example: Mark 5:7.

CANAANITE WOMAN

Matthew, drawing on Mark as a source, recounts the event of the Canaanite woman's faith. Matthew more fully describes the region as that of Tyre and Sidon. There is no mention of Jesus needing timeout. The Canaanite woman is not described as a Gentile. She bursts into the scene, shouting, "Have mercy on me, Lord, Son of David: my daughter is tormented by a demon" (Matt 15:22). We hear her plea and know that she recognises Jesus as Lord and Son of David. There is no mention of her falling down at his feet at this stage. The disciples feature in this version, urging Jesus to send her away. Obviously she is still shouting as the disciples comment on this. Jesus answers. It is not clear whether he is speaking to the disciples or to the woman, but surely the woman can hear him say, "I was sent only to the sheep of the house of Israel" (Matt 15:24). There is no ambiguity in Jesus' sense of his mission. Now she comes and worships him, saying, "Lord help me" (Matt 15:25). This posture of worship is used in Matthew only by those who recognise who Jesus is. These include the Magi, the leper and the synagogue official. Even in the face of being told by Jesus that "it is not fair to take the children's food and throw it to the dogs" (Matt 15:26), she has the swiftness of wit to reply, "Yes Lord, yet even the dogs eat the crumbs from the master's table." In Matthew's telling Jesus acclaims her faith: "Woman how great is your faith! Let this be done for you as you wish" (Matt 15:28). The addendum to this story is that the daughter is healed instantly.

INSPIRING EXAMPLE

The inclusion of this story in either of its forms is confusing and raises many questions. Whether it reflects a tension in these communities for the inclusion of Gentiles continues to be debated. This unnamed woman and mother is inspiring. She displays great faith and courage in the face of Jesus' rebuff and insult. Her challenge in reply brings about a change in Jesus' ministry, for he then journeys to the other side of the Sea of Galilee (Mark 7:31) and feeds the Gentiles (Mark 8:1–10; Matt 15:32–39).

PETER'S MOTHER-IN-LAW

The encounter with Peter's mother-in-law is more about observing what happens to her and her response. She is only introduced in her relationship to Peter and not by her own name. That she is in Peter's house may indicate that she is widowed and has no sons of her own. The three accounts of her tale (Mark 1:30–31; Matt 8:14–15; Luke 4:38–39) are short and similar, yet each has an element that indicates her fever is an evil spirit. In Matthew she is "cast down", suffering from a fever and the fever "lets go". In Mark she is lying down, the same verb is used as for the paralytic, and is suffering, as in Matthew, from a fever that "lets go". In Luke she is oppressed or held by a fever, and Jesus rebukes the fever as he would an evil spirit or demon. Luke's version is the most graphic in this regard. The accounts all indicate the link between ill health and the realm of evil spirits and demons. Jesus raises her in Mark, indicating her restoration to community and life for the Kingdom of God. Her immediate response in all three accounts is to serve, minister to (*diakoneō*) them/him. She is one of the women healed by Jesus who aids his mission.

> ...and she began to serve him.
> MATT 8:14–15
>
> ...and she began to serve them.
> MARK 1:30–31; LUKE 4:38–39

PILATE'S WIFE

Only in Matthew does Pilate's wife enter the scene of the trial of Jesus. She does not appear personally but sends a message. This cameo shows the influence of a wife on her husband. She is not named but linked to him as his wife. Pilate is sitting on the judgement seat, the *bema*, in a public place about to pass judgement. This is an urgent message delivered to her husband, saying, "Have nothing to do with that innocent man, for today I have suffered a great deal because of a dream about him" (Matt 27:19). The scene continues with Pilate asking the crowd to make a choice between Barabbas and Jesus, and when the call is for Jesus to be crucified Pilate washes his hands of the decision by saying, "I am innocent of this man's blood; see to it yourselves" (Matt 27:24) He has heeded the advice of his wife and distances himself from the judgement and Jesus but does not save him from the cross.

Pilate's wife was warned in a dream. In Matthew's Gospel account, dreams are mentioned six times: an angel of the Lord appears in a dream to Joseph to not be afraid of taking Mary as his wife (Matt 1:20); the Magi are warned in a dream not to go back to Herod; an angel of the Lord again appears to Joseph in a dream exhorting him to escape to Egypt with Mary and Jesus (Matt 2:13) and returns again to Joseph in a dream on the death of Herod to tell him to return his family home; on the way to Judea, there is another warning in a dream to Joseph not to go to Judea, so he changes course to Galilee (Matt 2:19); the final warning in a dream is that which came to Pilate's wife (Matt 27:19). The occurrences of dreams are the means of divine communication, which may indicate that the wife of Pilate was a Judean or a believer in God.

Left: Machaerus, site of Herod's palace where tradition remembers John the Baptist's death, Jordan
Below: The Dream of Pilate's Wife by Alphonse Francois

HERODIAS AND HER DAUGHTER

Herodias appears in three of the accounts of the gospel (Matt 14:3–12; Mark 6:17–29; Luke 3:19). In all three she is named as Herod's wife, having divorced from his brother, Philip. Herod is rebuked by John the Baptist for his marriage to Herodias, saying, "it is not lawful for you to have your brother's wife" (Mark 6:14; Matt 4:14). This is revealed in a flashback account of the death of John the Bapist in both Mark and Matthew. Luke's mention is more a side comment. Herodias is a woman powerfully placed, as is her daughter. Herodias' daughter is not named in the gospel accounts. Her name, Salome, is known from the *Antiquities of the Jews* written by Flavius Josephus (c.37–c.100CE).

On the occasion of Herod's birthday, Herodias' daughter is reported as dancing before Herod and his guests. Delighted by her performance, Herod offers to give her anything she wishes. At the suggestion of her mother, she requests the head of John the Baptist.

The actions of these two women illustrate the politics and power of the current regime. Herodias is portrayed as using her influence to protect her interests. Neither she nor her daughter appear as a likeable or exemplary character.

Above: 'Salome' by Titian

". . . but Herodias, their sister, was married to Herod [Philip], the son of Herod the Great, who was born of Mariamne, the daughter of Simon the high priest, who had a daughter, Salome; after whose birth Herodias took upon her to confound the laws of our country, and divorce herself from her husband while he was alive, and was married to Herod [Antipas], her husband's brother by the father's side; he was tetrarch of Galilee;"

FLAVIUS JOSEPHUS,
'ANTIQUITIES OF THE JEWS',
18.5.4

BUT WHEN HEROD'S BIRTHDAY CAME, THE DAUGHTER OF HERODIAS DANCED BEFORE THE COMPANY, AND SHE PLEASED HEROD SO MUCH THAT HE PROMISED ON OATH TO GRANT HER WHATEVER SHE MIGHT ASK. PROMPTED BY HER MOTHER, SHE SAID, 'GIVE ME THE HEAD OF JOHN THE BAPTIST HERE ON A PLATTER.'

MATT 14:6–8

DID YOU KNOW?

✠ Two senatorial votes laid the foundations for women to enter the visual landscape, allowing statues to be raised in their honour so that they would stand in public places and in temples alongside the men. In 35 BCE, the vote to allow statues to be raised in honour of Octavia (sister of Octavian who became Caesar Augustus) and Livia (wife of Octavian, later Augustus) is considered an innovation.[11] With only a couple of exceptions in all the preceding years, this was a decision in keeping with Augustus' use of propaganda via statuary especially to counter Cleopatra and Mark Anthony in the East. It was also a means of bestowing sacrosanctity and freedom from *tutela* (guardianship). The statues of Octavia and Livia presented them in Roman dress, further indicating the propaganda dimension of the power of the republic, the emperor and his family.

✠ In 16 BCE, Livia is the first to appear on provincial coins and lay the foundation of the model of virtue in the renewal of the republic.

Above: Head of Livia, 1st century, Ephesus, Selcuk Museum

Her images on the coins also conveyed the changing hairstyles, but more importantly, she was linked to Concordia (harmony) and Pietas (piety).

✠ In 9 BCE, the senatorial vote for the raising of statues of Livia are based on merit, which is a new perspective for Roman women.[12] On her birthday in 9 BCE, Livia was also honoured with the dedication of Ara Pacis Augustae, altar of the goddess of peace (Pax), built to honour Augustus' return to Rome from Gaul and Hispania. On the death of Drusus she was afforded further honours in consolation of her son's death. These honours affirmed the domestic and modest role of motherhood and also assured claims to succession. The images of Livia and Octavia raised the prominence of women in the public arena and may well have conveyed other messages to those who viewed them.

WIDOWS

Widows, specifically known as *almana* in Hebrew, were often synonymous with weeping, mourning and poverty. The *almana* were those widowed and left without social or economic support. Women left their family when they married, so the death of the husband would mean a tenuous link to his family, and the inheritance of land would pass from husband to son.

In the Old Testament there are frequent references to women in these terms such as in Job 27:15; 2 Sam 14:2; Lam 1:1 and Ruth 1:21. Earlier in this volume we met Anna the prophet in the Temple, who greeted Jesus as an infant and the Messiah. Anna was widowed early and childless and spent most of her life in the Temple (see Anna entry). Widows feature in the mission of Jesus and that of the early church. In Mark 12:40, Jesus rails against the scribes, saying, "they devour widows' houses". In the following verses he focuses on a widow placing two small coins into the treasury, "Truly I tell you this poor widow has put in more than all those who are contributing to the treasury."(Mark 12:43). In Acts 6:1–6, "seven men of good standing" are chosen to ensure the daily distribution of food to the widows. In Acts 9:36–42, a disciple called Tabitha, who is likely a widow among widows, is raised from the dead by Peter (see Tabitha entry). In the Letter of James, 1:27 advises that "to care for orphans and widows in their distress" is of prime importance in being righteous before God. 1 Timothy 5:3–16 affirms a widow who "left alone, has set her hope on God and continues in supplications and prayers night and day", who, like Anna or Tabitha, is doing good in every way.

WIDOW OF NAIN

When the Lord saw her, he had compassion for her and said to her, "Do not weep." Then he came forward and touched the bier, and the bearers stood still. And he said, "Young man, I say to you, rise!" The dead man sat up and began to speak, and Jesus gave him to his mother.
(Luke 7:13–15)

The widow of Nain appears only in Luke's Gospel (7:11–17). The story introduces her in relation to her only son who is being buried. This is the end of her life as she knows it. Jesus' compassion for her in raising her son restores her to her life in the community.

Below: The Court of the Women, temple model, Jerusalem

WOMEN IN THE PAULINE LETTERS

Above: Icon of Aquila and Prisca

JUNIA

Junia appears only once in the New Testament, in Paul's Letter to the Romans in one verse: 16:7. The great debate about Junia is whether the name recorded in the text is Junias (male), or Junia (female). The issue arises as the name is in the accusative "*Junian*".[13] Much of the argument centred on the assumption that this had to be a male name because there would not be a female apostle. The early manuscripts from Paul's time and the commentary of the Fathers do not seem to have this problem. The option of Junias was not introduced until the fourteenth century. Today, due to scholarly investigations in the 1970s, Junias has been relegated to a footnote and Junia is recognised as a woman, associated with Andronicus, perhaps his wife. The evidence of attested names in this period in Rome was instrumental in the decision. Peter Lampe located 250 occurences of 'Junia' in Rome alone.[14] The occurrence of Junius or Junianus the Greek form which could have abbreviated to Junias is rare enough to make this an unlikely option.

"MY RELATIVES"

Paul refers to both Andronicus and Junia as "my relatives". What does he mean by this? Are one or the other related to him by birth or extended family? More likely they are fellow Judeans. Paul reserves "brothers and sisters" for his followers in Christ.

"FELLOW PRISONERS"

This designation does not belong to Junia and Andronichus alone. Epaphras (Phm 1:23) and Aristarchus (Col 4:10) are described in this way too. The possibilities for this terminology include that they were in prison with Paul, or that they were in prison at some time or, in a metaphorical sense, were captives of Christ. There is simply not enough evidence to make a decision. Such an appellation does add to their closeness to Paul and association with sharing the suffering of Christ, so underlines them as faithful followers.

"PROMINENT AMONG THE APOSTLES"

Junia shares this affirmation with Andronichus. Debate arises around whether she is well known among the apostles or whether she is an apostle among apostles. Eldon Epp (2005) concludes she is an apostle and quotes John Chrysostum (c.349–407) more than once.

> Greet Andronicus and Junia, my relatives and fellow prisoners; they are prominent among the apostles, and they were in Christ before I was.
> ROMANS 16:7*

> "Even to be an apostle is great, but also to be prominent among them… — consider how wonderful a song of honour that is. For they were prominent because of their works, because of their successes. Glory be! How great the wisdom of this woman that she was even deemed worthy of the apostle's title."
> John Chrysostum (c.349–407)
> *In ep ad Romanos* 31.2

Earlier the criteria for an apostle were listed as witnessing the appearance of the Risen Christ and receiving a divine call or commission (see Mary Magdalene page 12). There is no description of any criteria here, but rather they are simply named as apostles. The description as "prominent among the apostles" is only afforded them and may reveal their contribution to the formation of the community in Rome.

"IN CHRIST BEFORE I WAS"

Junia and Andronichus are recognised as being "in Christ" before Paul. This could indicate that they were Palestinian Jews and members of the Jerusalem Church. Their association with Rome and their naming as prominent among the apostles suggests their participation and leadership in the proclamation of the good news in Rome.

Left: Plancia Magna 2nd century, Perge, Antalya Archaelogical Museum

PRISCA (PRISCILLA)

Prisca and her husband, Aquila, are a leadership couple and close friends of Paul. In Paul's letters he refers to her as Prisca. Paul uses her full name, giving her respect. In Acts she is referred to by the diminutive of her name, perhaps indicating familiarity but also potentially lessening her status.

PRISCA IN PAUL'S LETTERS

The first reference to Prisca and Aquila is in the greetings Paul sends from Ephesus to the Corinthians. His greetings are joined by those of Aquila and Prisca "together with the church in their house". Together, Aquila and Prisca offer hospitality in their house to the community of faith and likely the leaders of the assemblies. In Paul's Letter to the Romans, we are given a glimpse of the strong bond between Paul and this couple when he asks the Romans to "Greet Prisca and Aquila who work with me in Christ Jesus, and who risked their necks for my life" (Rom 3–5). They are not only co-workers but have risked their lives for him and the sake of the gospel. Further greetings are extended to Prisca and Aquila in the second letter to Timothy (2 Tim 4:19). Note that Prisca's name has moved to be the first mentioned in both Romans and 2 Timothy. A similar pattern emerges in Acts.

PRISCILLA IN ACTS

In Acts 18, we hear of Paul arriving in Corinth from Athens. There he meets Aquila, a Judean and a native of Pontus (Acts 18:2). He has fled with his wife Priscilla from Rome (Italy) because the Emperor Claudius commanded all Judeans to leave the city. We learn that Paul shared the trade of tent-making with them and they worked and lived together (Acts 18:3). So it is in Corinth that the friendship is forged, and we are advised that "after staying there a considerable time, Paul said farewell to the believers and sailed for Syria, accompanied by Priscilla and Aquila" (Acts 18:18).

Once they arrived in Ephesus, Paul left them there, and they appear to have set up their house church. It is possible that Prisca and Aquila had a shop in the Tetragonos agora (commercial marketplace), where they continued their trade with Paul working with them.

Encountering another preacher, Apollos from Alexandria, actively and enthusiastically proclaiming Jesus and the Way of the Lord, they take it upon themselves to instruct him "for he knew only the baptism of John". It is clear that both Priscilla and Aquila are engaged in the instruction of Apollos. With her name first, Priscilla takes the lead.

Below: Temple of Apollo on the ancient site of Corinth, Built c. 540 BCE

DID YOU KNOW?

✢ Women are recognised and honoured for benefaction and public office in the time of the Roman Empire, especially in Asia Minor (today's Turkey). Although such honours were less frequent for women than men, they did include offices of the highest order, including *stephanophorus* or "crown bearer", who could be responsible for sacrifices and coinage. In some instances women held the title in their own right, while at other times they were attributed the office through their husbands. Marcia Aurelia Glaucia, a woman in Tralles, was recorded on a coin as a clerk (*grammateus*), and Flavia Asclepia of Germe, near Dorylaeum, held the office of councillor (*strategos*).[15] Iulia Menogenis shared titles with her husband and also held some in her own right. She is honoured for providing colonnades for the city of Thyatira, while her husband furnished the city with buildings.[16]

✢ These few examples are representative of the ability of women to hold positions of honour and also show that there was a level of acceptance of women in public leadership and benefactor roles. Phoebe in Romans 16:2 is noted as "benefactor", a title that is broader than her role in the Pauline mission yet appears to operate within that also. Leadership in Pauline house church communities by women could only have been enhanced by the acceptance in the wider community of women in public office.

Left: A stele from Laodikeia depicts standing figures of a male and female with a mirror between their heads. The inscription honours Meltine daughter of Damas, Denizli Archaeological Museum.
Below: Mithradates and Mazeus Gate to the Tetragonos Agora (Commercial Market), in situ 1st century CE, Ephesus.

PHOEBE

Phoebe is introduced as "our sister" which designates her at least as a member of the community of faith using the household language that is a hallmark of Paul. Here the particular reference likely indicates she has a leadership role. Apphia is likewise designated in this way in the Letter to Philemon (1:2). Phoebe is also named "deacon of the church /assembly at Cenchreae". With these appelations, Phoebe is affirmed by Paul as a significant woman and leader in the community of faith.

Cenchreae (Kenchreai) is one of two ports governed by Corinth: Cenchreae (Kenchreai) lay to the east servicing the Aegean and Asia Minor; Lechaeum (Lechaeion) was situated to the north, linking to the Adriatic and Italy. The ports were thought to be named after the children of Poseidon and Piriene: Leches and Kenchias.

"DEACON" AND "BENEFACTOR"

Paul recommends Phoebe to the community in Rome as both deacon (*diakonos*) and benefactor or patron (*prostatis*). This implies she is the letter carrier, as Paul asks the Romans to welcome her. Phoebe is announced in a similar manner to Timothy in 1 Thess 3:2: "our brother and deacon for God". Paul commends Phoebe as being a benefactor or patron of "many and of myself". There is no further elaboration. The inference is that she is a woman of means who supports Paul financially as well as through hospitality and ministry to the community.

Phoebe appears in Chapter 16 of the Letter to the Romans along with Prisca, Mary, Junia Tryphaena and Tryphosa, Persis, Rufus' mother, Julia and Nereus's sister.

DID YOU KNOW ?

✠ In August 2016, Pope Francis created a commission to study whether women might serve as deacons in the Catholic Church. Known as "The Study Commission on the Women's Diaconate", the commission members include equal numbers of male and female experts: six priests, four laywomen and two women religious.

Below: Marble portrait head of a female, likely from Cenchreae 120–140 CE, Corinth Archaeological Museum

"I COMMEND TO YOU OUR SISTER PHOEBE, A DEACON OF THE CHURCH AT CENCHREAE, SO THAT YOU MAY WELCOME HER IN THE LORD AS IS FITTING FOR ALL THE SAINTS, AND HELP HER IN WHATEVER SHE MAY REQUIRE FROM YOU, FOR SHE HAS BEEN A BENEFACTOR OF MANY AND OF MYSELF AS WELL."

ROM 16:1–2

WOMEN IN ROME

Along with Phoebe, Prisca and Junia (already separately listed) Paul sends greetings to Mary, Junia Tryphaena and Tryphosa, Persis, Rufus' mother, Julia and Nereus's sister.

"Greet Mary who has worked hard for you." (Rom 16:6).
"Greet Tryphaena and Tryphosa, workers in the Lord." (Rom 16:12).
"Greet the beloved Persis, who has worked hard in the Lord." (Rom 16:12).

Mary, Tryphaena and Tryphosa and Persis are all described using derivatives of the same word for work, *kopiaō,* which has the sense of toil and labour. They do not share the title of "fellow worker in Christ" that is given to Urbanus (Rom 16:9). Persis is further noted as "the beloved" and is the only woman to be described this way. Both Epaenetus and Stachys are called "my beloved" (Rom 16:5, 9), and Ampliatus is called "my beloved in the Lord" (Rom 16:8). Rufus' mother is "a mother to me also" (Rom 16:13). Clearly she is not Paul's mother but treats him like a son. Julia and Nereus' sister are included in greetings (Rom 16:15) with no other information.

This group of named women are significant in the mission of Paul. They are known and greeted in the letter and named for their ministry, collaboration in the work of the mission and contribution to the communities of faith. These are beloved women who offer hospitality and who work hard for the Lord.

Left: Aphphia inscription from Ankara dated to 1st to 3rd century CE. Note also wool symbols on stele.

Below: Church of Laodikeia, near Denizli, Turkey

OTHER WOMEN OF THE PAULINE HOUSEHOLD COMMUNITIES

APPHIA

Apphia appears in the beginning of the Letter of Paul to Philemon (Phlm 2). She is addressed as "the sister" in a similar way that Timothy is addressed as "the brother" (Phlm 1). The relationship between Philemon, Apphia and Archippus is not clear. Philemon is likely the leader of the Colossian community assembly and appears to share that leadership with Apphia and Archippus. The "church in your house" is also greeted, indicating that this may be Philemon's house. Apphia is sometimes thought to have been Philemon's wife, which is possible, and Archippus may have been their son. His mention in Colossians 4:17 is that he should see to his ministry (*diakonia*). This gathering place for the Christ followers is likely in Colossae, based on the number of shared greetings of both the Letter to Philemon and that to the Colossians. Apphia and Philemon may have operated in a similar way to Prisca and Aquila, as a married couple on mission.

The name Apphia has its origins in Anatolia and is often attested in inscriptions in Caria, Lydia and Phrygia.[17] There are instances of inscriptions with Apphia in the area of Colossae, yet they are dated to later periods than to the time of writing of the letter. The closest in time is likely one from Hierapolis, a neighbouring city to Colossae. Dated to the Flavian period 69–96 CE, the inscription names Apphia the daughter of Zeuxis as instigating a series of dedications.[18]

CHLOE

When Paul sends his first letter to the Corinthians, he reports that he has heard of strife among them from Chloe's people (literally "those of Chloe"): "It has been reported about you, my brothers and sisters, by those of Chloe, that there is strife among you" (1 Cor 1:11). Chloe is likely head of household and possibly a leader of a house church. There are no more details about her, yet her name was clearly known to the Pauline community in Corinth.

EUODIA AND SYNTYCHE

Euodia and Syntyche are mentioned in Paul's letter to the Philippians (4:2–3). They are described as having struggled beside him in the work of the gospel along with Clement and the rest of his co-workers. Being engaged in the struggle with Paul indicates they have been on the front lines in the establishment of the community in Philippi. Here Paul's reference to them is in terms of some disagreement between them and he exhorts them to be of the same mind in the Lord.

NYMPHA

Among the greetings at the end of the Letter to the Colossians are those to the brothers and sisters in Laodikeia and to Nympha and the church in her house (Col 4:15). Despite issues with whether the name is in fact that of a male (Nymphas), the pronoun indicates "her house", and inscriptional evidence weighs in for the feminine form of the name. Nympha, then, is another of the women named as leader of a Pauline community. There is no description of her role; however, as with other women she is likely a patron offering her house for the assembly of the community.

DID YOU KNOW?

✠ The ancient site of the city of Laodikeia in Turkey is currently being excavated and has yielded evidence of 7 churches plus a peristyle house with oratory, a chapel and a baptistery dating to the Early Byzantine period, fourth to the sixth centuries.[19] The proliferation of building in that period follows the decree by Emperor Constantine in 313 CE, which gave freedom to Christianity to practice, and to the outcome of the First Council held in Nicea in 325 and a regional synod at Laodikeia c.341–281.

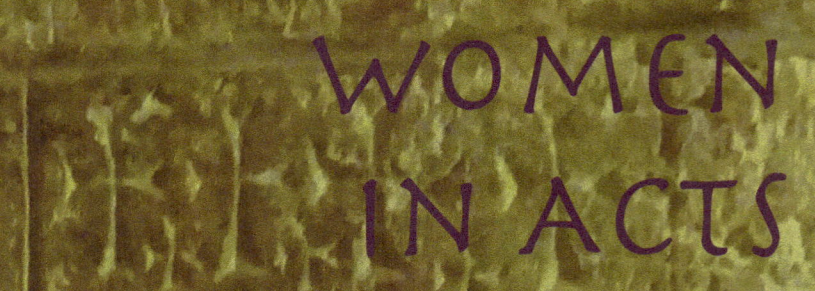

WOMEN IN ACTS

Above: Icon of Lydia in the modern baptistery outside the ancient site of Philippi, Greece, 2012

Background: Pilgrim crosses in Church of the Holy Sepulchre, Jerusalem

LYDIA

Lydia is named only in three verses in the Book of Acts (16:14–15, 40). In these few lines, Luke, the attributed author of the Book of Acts, paints her as a significant woman of faith, the first person baptised in Europe and one who leads a house church in Philippi. Her actions are inspirational to women and men called to leadership and ministry in the church through the ages.

SO WHO IS LYDIA?

There is little known of Lydia. In the Book of Acts she is first encountered unnamed in a group of women who are gathered by the river on the outskirts of the ancient city of Philippi (Acts 16:13). In those days Philippi was a city of Macedonia (today this area is part of Greece). Paul has travelled across the ocean from Troas in Asia Minor (today's Turkey) in response to a plea in a dream by a Macedonian: "Come over to Macedonia and help us" (Acts 16:9).

Travelling via Samothrace and Neapolis, Paul and his companions arrive in Philippi, which is a "leading city in the district of Macedonia and a Roman colony" (Acts 16:12). It is on the Sabbath that Paul and his followers seek out a prayer place by the river outside the gate of the city.

The mention of a place of prayer along with the terminology of gathering that is given to the women could indicate that this is at least a synagogue equivalent in Philippi. Yet Luke has been vague in his account, perhaps preferring to maintain a semblance of the usual pattern of Paul going first to the synagogue.[20] The posture of sitting is consistent with listening to a rabbi. In Acts, Paul regularly seeks out the synagogue when he arrives in a new city, but here it is a gathering of women. This is the only reference to a gathering of women in the New Testament.

LYDIA THE MERCHANT

Lydia is also described as having come from Thyatira and as a

> A certain woman named Lydia, a worshipper of God, was listening to us; she was from the city of Thyatira and a dealer in purple cloth. The Lord opened her heart to listen eagerly to what was said by Paul.
> ACTS 16:14

Above: Modern mosaic depicting Paul's dream of a Macedonian entreating him to come and help him. Kavala, Greece
Below: Madder root

merchant dealing in purple cloth (Acts 16:14). The title used here in the Greek for merchant in purple, *porphuropolis,* can mean dealing in purple cloth or goods dyed with purple or with the dye itself. Thyatira is a city in the province of Lydia in Asia Minor well regarded for its vegetable dye trade, especially from the Madder Root (red dye). Lydia may well have learned the dye trade while in Thyatira. The Book of Revelation also refers to Thyatira as one of the seven churches (Rev. 1:11; 2:18; 2:24). The coincidence of Lydia's name and the province being the same is often thought to indicate she was a slave, known by her ethnicity. Inscriptional evidence of elite women known by this name brings this assumption into question. Lydia's status as a merchant in the purple trade, named without a husband, may indicate she is a widowed freed woman or perhaps a single woman. She is definitely portrayed as a business woman in her own right, as Lydia is in charge of a household and for that she must have freed status either as a freeborn or freed slave. Described by her work rather than by her family name, Lydia is unlikely a Roman citizen.

The many unknowns about Lydia have led some scholars to think that she was a member of the elite, especially with the mention of purple trade. The expensive purple dye of the murex mollusk, also known as Tyrian purple, was used by emperors for their togas, and those dealing in this had to be members of the imperial household.

At the ancient site of Philippi in the newly built Baptistery, the icon of Lydia shows her clothed in red, furthering her connection with Thyatira and indicating her association with a red-purple rather than the expensive purple dye trade.

LYDIA'S LISTENING HEART AND HOSPITALITY

Lydia is portrayed as one with an openness to hear the word of God. She is described as "a worshipper of God" and as "listening to us" (Acts 16:14). The narrative moves quickly to the baptism of her and her household. This is an established pattern in Acts where, upon hearing the good news proclaimed by Paul, the householder and all her/his household are baptised. Lydia adds to this her urging of them to come and stay at her house. Such was her urging that "she prevailed upon us". So Paul and his companions go to stay at her home, which is the first foundation in Europe.

Lydia is one of the few female Lukan characters who speak. Her words indicate that she is a woman of hospitality and leadership. She remains an inspiration, as it is possible to imitate her response to her baptismal call. Some scholars believe she is a "type" rather than an actual person. Whichever she is, Lydia offers an insight into those moved by the gospel proclaimed by Paul to join the Christ followers, offering hospitality to the travelling missionaries and nurturing and strengthening believers in their homes. The baptismal call was to women and men alike, and they took their call to ministry seriously and in faith. Lydia is inspirational as an example of one open to God and enthusiastic in her response, acting immediately to affirm her belief and living out her faith using all her resources to support and encourage others to follow the good news.

Lydia's story with Paul also pairs with Tabitha's story with Peter. A patterning of Jewish and Gentile

> "On the sabbath day we went outside the gate by the river, where we supposed there was a place of prayer; and we sat down and spoke to the women who had gathered there."
> ACTS 16:13

spread of the good news. Both Lydia and Tabitha are engaged in the clothing and dye trade and weave skills into their ministry.

DID YOU KNOW?

✠ The Greek goddess Athena provided women with the attributes for weaving. Her equivalent in Rome was Minerva.[21] Both weaving and spinning were considered sacred duties symbolically linked with spinning the thread of life. The youngest of the three fates, Clotho, was responsible for spinning the fate of human existence. With such sacred duties, it is easy to understand that wool and weaving were considered signs of virtue for women. Symbols of distaff, wool basket and wool were common on grave stones (steles) and funerary monuments. In the elite houses in Ephesus, elaborate distaffs were found on display in the house to show the virtue of the women.

Left: Baptismal site in the river just outside the ancient site of Philippi, Greece

TABITHA (DORCAS)

TABITHA NAMED AS DISCIPLE

Tabitha is the only woman in the New Testament to be named "disciple"(*mathetria*) using the feminine form of the word used for Jesus' disciples (*mathetes*). Tabitha appears to be a widow and is known for her "good works and acts of charity". Her skills in making tunics and clothing are testament to her honour and industry (Acts 9:39).

She is well known to the disciples, who send two men for Peter from nearby Lydda in a manner that recalls Jesus being invited to the home of Lazarus and Jairus. As Peter arrives it is "all the widows" who stand beside him. Peter continues to be cast imitating Jesus when he clears the room and raises Tabitha from death. The addition here is that Peter knelt down and prayed, showing that his power to heal came from God.

WIDOW AMONG WIDOWS

Tabitha will continue her good works among the community. Tabitha is likely a widow herself among widows, building a community among the marginalised and engaging them in her good works.

> "TABITHA, GET UP."
> THEN SHE OPENED HER EYES, AND SEEING PETER, SHE SAT UP.
> HE GAVE HER HIS HAND AND HELPED HER UP.
> THEN CALLING THE SAINTS AND WIDOWS,
> HE SHOWED HER TO BE ALIVE.
> THIS BECAME KNOWN THROUGHOUT JOPPA,
> AND MANY BELIEVED IN THE LORD.
> ACTS 9:40–42

SAPPHIRA

Sapphira holds an ignoble place in Acts for her complicity with her husband in not sharing everything in common. The story of Sapphira is recounted as occurring after Pentecost in Jerusalem. As Peter and John and the apostles preached boldly with the power of the Spirit, they established the new community of Christ. The believers actively shared everything, selling land and houses and giving the proceeds to the apostles for distribution "to each as any had need" (Acts 4:34–35). Ananias, Sapphira's husband, sells a piece of land with her consent (Acts 5:1). Ananias conspires to hold back some of the proceeds and his wife agrees. There is little detail of either character. They appear for a specific walk-on role to show the consequence of not sharing possessions. The result is that each in turn falls down dead. Sapphira is buried next to her husband. They are dead to this community. Sapphira's complicity in this rests in her choice to give consent to the sale of the land and to agree to hold back some of the proceeds. She is not a passive character and acts to elucidate women's responsibility. This exemplary tale delivers a warning to those who are not fully committed.

OTHER WOMEN IN ACTS

There are a number of women named in Acts for whom we have little other than their names. That they are named indicates that they were sufficiently well known in the community to be recorded by name.

DAMARIS

In Athens, one woman, Damaris, is named as joining the believers: "But some of them joined him and became believers, including Dionysius the Areopagite and a woman named Damaris, and others with them" (Acts 17:34).

DRUSILLA

Drusilla is the wife of Marcus Antonius Felix (referred to as Felix in Acts 23:24, 26; 24:22, 24, 25; 25:14), Roman procurator or governor of the Judean province 52–58 CE. She is described as a Judean.

Earlier, Paul was brought before Felix in Caesarea (Acts 24:1–23) to make his case, but Felix, "who was well informed of the Way", adjourned the hearing (Acts 24:22). Drusilla accompanies Felix when he comes and calls for Paul, while he is in custody at Caesarea, to speak about his faith in Jesus: "Some days later when Felix came with his wife Drusilla, who was Jewish, he sent for Paul and heard him speak concerning faith in Christ Jesus" (Acts 24:24).

We know nothing of what Drusilla may have said or her influence, yet the narrative reports that "… as he discussed justice, self-control, and the coming judgment, Felix became frightened and said, 'Go away for the present; when I have an opportunity, I will send for you'" (Acts 24:25). He appears to be as Pilate with Jesus: also warned by his wife, not wanting to make a judgement on this man for fear of the Judeans and to maintain order and for his own sake. What part Drusilla played in his decision is not clear, but she was present, and Felix left Paul in custody for the next governor, Porcius Festus.

BERNICE

Bernice, like Drusilla, is involved in the events of the trials of Paul. She is the wife of King Agrippa, who comes to Caesarea to welcome Porcius Festus, who succeeds Felix (Acts 25:13). Paul has already appeared before Festus and appealed to be heard by the Emperor so is in custody when Agrippa and Bernice arrive. Agrippa requests to hear Paul's case. Bernice is with him and explicitly named (Acts 25:13, 23–4; 26:30–31). At the end of Paul's testimony, "the king got up, and with him the governor and Bernice and those who had been seated with them" (Acts 26:30) and as they left they said to one another, "This man is doing nothing to deserve death or imprisonment."(Acts 26:31). Bernice was part of this conversation that concluded that Paul could have been freed if he had not appealed to the Emperor.

DID YOU KNOW?

✠ The followers of Jesus were also known as "the Way". This designation is found three times in Acts. The first is when Saul (later to be known as Paul) requested letters from the high priest to take to the synagogues at Damascus, giving him permission to arrest and bind any women or men of the Way that he found there and bring them back to Jerusalem (Acts 9:2). The second occurrence was in Ephesus, where "no little disturbance broke out concerning the Way" (Acts 19:23). The silversmiths gathered in an angry mob protesting against their loss of sales of silver shrines of Artemis, which they attributed to the preaching of Paul and his companions. The third is Felix, the governor of Judea, speaking of the Way when Paul is being brought before him in Caesarea.

Left: Mosaic depicting a Roman woman

MORE WOMEN

There are many more women, too many for this volume. These include the women married to seven brothers in succession (Matt 22:23–30; Mark 12:18–25; Luke 20:27–36), the servant girl who accuses Peter (Mark 14:66–69; Luke 22:56–57), the woman caught in adultery (John 8:3–11) and the woman bent over for eighteen years (Luke 13:11–16).

In 1 Timothy within a passage regarding deacons (1 Tim 3:8–13) women are instructed in a similar way to deacons, "to be serious, not slanderers, but temperate, faithful in all things" (1 Tim 3:11). This is often considered to imply that women were once deacons and are thought to have been essential to assisting women in the ritual of baptism. Along with Prisca, the following women are noted in the Pastoral Letters.

LOIS AND EUNICE

Eunice is the mother of Timothy who is the beloved brother of Paul and his co-worker in the mission. Lois is his grandmother. It is these two women who are attributed to nurturing and teaching Timothy in the faith.[22] In the Second Letter to Timothy, he is affirmed for his sincere faith. In Acts 16:1–3, Timothy is introduced as having a Jewish mother and Greek father. There is inference of matrilineal descent, yet Timothy has not been circumcised. Perhaps this is because his father is a Greek. Both Lois and Eunice have Greek names and may have adopted these in the diaspora. Paul has Timothy circumcised so he will be more acceptable to the Jewish communities. Further affirmation for the first teachers appears at the end of 2 Timothy:

> But as for you, continue in what you have learned and firmly believed, knowing from whom you learned it, and how from childhood you have known the sacred writings that are able to instruct you for salvation through faith in Christ Jesus.
> (2 Tim 3:14–15)

This valued practice of parents and grandparents passing on the faith and sharing the scriptures is as important today as in the first century. Mothers and grandmothers, along with fathers and grandfathers, are the first teachers of children in the home, not only of practical living skills but of religious beliefs and values.

CLAUDIA

Claudia appears in the greetings of the second letter of Paul to Timothy (2 Tim 4:21). She is listed as sending greetings along with Eubulus, Pudens and Linus. As such, she is indicated as a significant person of the mission, possibly providing accommodation for travelling missionaries or hosting community assemblies in her house.

> I am reminded of
> your sincere faith,
> a faith that lived first in your
> grandmother Lois
> and your mother Eunice
> and now, I am sure, lives in you.
> 2 Tim 1:5

DID YOU KNOW?

✠ The account of the woman caught in adultery appears in the Gospel of John, yet in many modern volumes it is bracketed, meaning there are doubts to it being original to John. The doubts come from the investigation of the ancient manuscripts on which the received text in the canon is based. The studies show that the account of this woman is only in manuscripts dated to the fifth century CE or later.[23] It does not appear in the earliest and most reliable manuscripts. In addition, this story does not consistently appear in the same place in the manuscripts where it is evident. There are manuscripts that include it in the Gospel of Luke either after 21:38 or at the end after 24:53. Others locate it in John, at the end after 21:25 or at 7:36.

CONCLUSION

The primary hope for this *Friendly Guide to Women in the New Testament* is that it provides ready access in intelligible language to the women who are encountered in the pages and stories of the New Testament. Beyond this primary hope, there is the prospect that engagement with this introductory information will lead to further investigation and reflection on the women who were significant in the Jesus movement from the beginning. These women continue to inspire women today in the way they live out the gospel.

The world today is greatly changed from the first century and the Church structure and tradition has grown and developed since those early days. Yet in some ways there are considerable similarities. Only some of the women are named and hold particular significance. Many are unnamed, and some of these become legendary for their acts of faith. Some are with Jesus or drawn to Jesus through disciples or followers of Jesus from the beginning and stay to the end, but many others come in and out as life, energy and opportunity ebb and flow. Not all are inspirational. Each of these women encountered Jesus himself or through others. For many, their lives radically changed through this encounter. That opportunity is still there for everyone today who has the openness of heart of Lydia, the yes of Mary, the love of Mary Magdalene, or the generosity of the widow who placed two small coins, all she had, into the treasury.

Women today take their place in ministry and service at many levels of the Church; some are teachers of the faith in primary, secondary and tertiary educational facilities, sharing their gifts and talents in communities of faith and the wider world. We celebrate particular women who become saints like St Mary of the Cross MacKillop here in Australia. In the first century language of Paul, all followers of Jesus were addressed in his letters as "saints" or "holy ones". This is an active encouragement to all the faithful to live out their lives in holiness and in proclaiming the good news.

The end of this book is indeed a beginning and an invitation. It is the beginning of your further exploration of the women in the New Testament and an invitation to write your own story of faith in your own corner of the world today.

BIBLIOGRAPHY

Ascough, Richard S. *Lydia: Paul's Cosmopolitan Hostess.* Collegeville: Liturgical Press, 2009.

Bauckham, Richard. *Gospel Women: Studies of the Named Women in the Gospels London*: T&T Clark, 2002.

Brock, Ann Graham. *Mary Magdalene, the First Apostle: The Struggle for Authority.* Cambridge: Harvard University Press, 2003.

Canavan, Rosemary. "Weaving Threads: Clothing in Colossae." In *Fragments of Colossae: Sifting through the Traces*, edited by Alan H. Cadwallader, 111–34. Hindmarsh: ATF Press, 2015.

Coloe, Mary L. "The Mother of Jesus: A Woman Possessed." In *Character Studies in the Fourth Gospel,* edited by Steven A. Hunt, D. Francois Tolmie and Ruben Zimmerman, 202–13. Tübingen: Mohr Siebeck, 2013.

Coloe, Mary L. "The Woman of Samaria: Her Characterisation, Narrative and Theological Significance." In *Characters and Characterisation in the Gospel of John,* edited by Christopher W. Skinner, 182–86. London: T&T Clark, 2013.

Epp, Eldon Jay. *Junia: The First Woman Apostle.* Minneapolis: Fortress Press, 2005.

Flory, Marleen B. "Livia and the History of Public Honorific Statues for Women in Rome." *Transactions of the American Philological Association* 123 (1993): 287–308.

Top: Young woman from Crete 69–96, Istanbul Museum
Middle: Livia 1st century Ephesus, Selçuk Museum
Bottom: Woman 1st century Istanbul Museum

Getty-Sullivan, Mary Ann. *Women in the New Testament.* Collegeville: The Liturgical Press, 2001.

Gooder, Paula. *Searching for Meaning: An Introduction to Interpreting the New Testament.* Louisville: Westminster John Knox Press, 2009.

Huttner, Ulrich. *Early Christianity in the Lycus Valley.* Translated by David Green. Leiden and Boston: Brill, 2013.

MacMullen, Ramsay. "Women in Public in the Roman Empire." *Historia* (1980): 208–18.

Meyers, Carol. *Women in Scripture: A Dictionary of Named and Unnamed Women in the Hebrew Bible, the Apocryphal/Deuterocanonical Books, and the New Testament.* Grand Rapids: William B. Eerdmans Publishing Company, 2000.

Moloney, Francis J. *Woman First among the Faithful: A New Testament Study.* Blackburn: Dove Communications, 1984.

Simsek, Celal. *Church of Laodikeia: Christianity in the Lykos Valley.* Denizli: Denizli Metropolitan Municipality & Professor Celal Simsek, 2015.

van Bremen, Riet. *The Limits of Participation: Women and Civic Life in the Greek East in the Hellenistic and Roman Periods.* Amsterdam: J. C. Gieben, 1996.

ENDNOTES

1. Mary L. Coloe, "The Mother of Jesus: A Woman Possessed," in *Character Studies in the Fourth Gospel*, ed. Steven A. Hunt, D. Francois Tolmie, and Ruben Zimmerman (Tübingen: Mohr Siebeck, 2013), 202–13.

2. For further information on qualifications for apostleship see Ann Graham Brock, *Mary Magdalene, the First Apostle: The Struggle for Authority* (Cambridge: Harvard University Press, 2003), 6–9.

3. Richard Bauckham, *Gospel Women: Studies of the Named Women in the Gospels* (London: T&T Clark, 2002), 203–23.

4. Ibid., 204–12.

5. Ibid.

6. Hegesippus *apud* Eusebius, Hist. Eccl. 3.11; 3.32.6; 4.22.4 as quoted by Richard Bauckham. Ibid., 208.

7. Francis J. Moloney, *Woman First among the Faithful: A New Testament Study* (Blackburn: Dove Communications, 1984), 75.

8. Mary L. Coloe, "The Woman of Samaria: Her Characterisation, Narrative and Theological Significance," in *Characters and Characterisation in the Gospel of John*, ed. Christopher W. Skinner (London: T&T Clark, 2013), 182–96.

9. Ibid., 194–96.

10. Elizabeth Struthers Malbon, "Syrophoenician Woman," in *Women in Scripture: A Dictionary of Named and Unnamed Women in the Hebrew Bible, the Apocryphal/Deuterocanonical Books, and the New Testament*, ed. Carol Meyers (Grand Rapids: William B. Eerdmans Publishing Company, 2000), 426–27.

11. Marleen B. Flory, "Livia and the History of Public Honorific Statues for Women in Rome," *Transactions of the American Philological Association* 123 (1993): 287–308.

12. Ibid.

13. For a detailed explanation regarding Junia or Junias see Eldon Jay Epp, *Junia: The First Woman Apostle* (Minneapolis: Fortress Press, 2005), 23–29.

14. Bauckham, *Gospel Women*, 167–68.

15. Ramsay MacMullen, "Women in Public in the Roman Empire," *Historia* (1980): 208–18.

16. Riet van Bremen, *The Limits of Participation: Women and Civic Life in the Greek East in the Hellenistic and Roman Periods*. (Amsterdam: J. C. Gieben, 1996), 117.

17. Ulrich Huttner, *Early Christianity in the Lycus Valley*, trans. David Green (Leiden and Boston: Brill, 2013), 84–85.

18. Ibid., 85.

19. Celal Simsek, *Church of Laodikeia: Christianity in the Lykos Valley* (Denizli: Denizli Metropolitan Municipality & Professor Celal Simsek, 2015), 21.

20. Richard Ascough offers provides insight to the place of prayer. See Richard S. Ascough, *Lydia: Paul's Cosmopolitan Hostess* (Collegeville: Liturgical Press, 2009), 86–90.

21. Rosemary Canavan, "Weaving Threads: Clothing in Colossae," in *Fragments of Colossae: Sifting through the Traces*, ed. Alan H. Cadwallader (Hindmarsh: ATF Press, 2015), 111–34.

22. Mary Ann Getty-Sullivan, *Women in the New Testament* (Collegeville: The Liturgical Press, 2001), 148.

23. Paula Gooder, *Searching for Meaning: An Introduction to Interpreting the New Testament* (Louisville: Westminster John Knox Press, 2009), 52–53.

Above: Young Faustina 2nd century, Perge-Antalya Archaelogical Museum

www.ingramcontent.com/pod-product-compliance
Lightning Source LLC
Chambersburg PA
CBHW061059170426
43199CB00025B/2939